Rousas John
Rushdoony

To Be As God

A Study of Modern Thought since the Marquis de Sade

Vallecito, California

Ross House Books
PO Box 67
Vallecito, CA 95251
www.rosshousebooks.org

Library of Congress Catalog Card Number: 2003092088
ISBN:1-879998-38-6

Printed in the United States of America

Other books by
Rousas John Rushdoony

The Institutes of Biblical Law, Vol. I
The Institutes of Biblical Law, Vol. II, Law & Society
The Institutes of Biblical Law, Vol. III, The Intent of the Law
Systematic Theology (2 volumes)
Chariots of Prophetic Fire
Hebrews, James & Jude
The Gospel of John
Larceny in the Heart
The Biblical Philosophy of History
The Mythology of Science
Thy Kingdom Come
Foundations of Social Order
This Independent Republic
The Nature of the American System
The "Atheism" of the Early Church
The Messianic Character of American Education
The Philosophy of the Christian Curriculum
Christianity and the State
Salvation and Godly Rule
Romans & Galatians
God's Plan for Victory
Politics of Guilt and Pity
Roots of Reconstruction
The One and the Many
Revolt Against Maturity
By What Standard?
Law & Liberty

For a complete listing of available books
by Rousas John Rushdoony and other
Christian reconstructionists, contact:

ROSS HOUSE BOOKS
PO Box 67 * Vallecito, CA 95251
www.rosshousebooks.org

Table of Contents

Foreword

This work was one of a number of incomplete manuscripts my father, Rousas John Rushdoony, left behind at his death in 2001. Those who were conversant with him in his last years will remember his references to his "study on modern thought since the Marquis de Sade." He considered this one of his more important works and planned to write "just a few more pages" to complete it.

My father frequently explained the destructive nature of man and his culture in terms of Proverbs 8:35-36:

> For whoso findeth me findeth life, and shall obtain favor of the Lord.
> But he that sinneth against me wrongeth his own soul: all they that hate me love death.

My father recognized something many modern Christians do not, that non-Christian man and his culture are at war with God. Man in rebellion against God is still trying to cash-in Satan's bogus promise to Eve in the Garden of Eden: "Ye shall be as gods, knowing [i.e., determining for yourselves] good and evil" (Gen. 3:5).

One of the first examples of this conscious warring against God was the Tower of Babel. In Genesis 11:3 the builders of Babel are quoted as saying:

> Go to, let us build us a city, and a tower, whose top may reach unto heaven; and let us make us a name, lest we be scattered abroad upon the face of the whole earth.

Often, in telling Biblical stories to children, we so trivialize their meaning we lose their message. As interesting as this story is to children, it is about adults and a message to God's people about how adults try to defy God. One of the ways we trivialize this account is in assuming the people were actually trying to get to heaven, as if reaching up to God was their goal.

The builders of Babel had no desire to find God. God is not mentioned in their plans. The ambition of the builders of Babel was to build a city, a civilization, a culture, and a monument to represent their power. Their desire to reach unto heaven was a desire to rival heaven, to be a manifestation of heaven on earth, supreme in power and glory; it was about rivaling God with a political and cultural center. Babel was to be a manifestation of this alternative heaven on earth; the city and tower would display their greatness. The builders of Babel wanted to make a name for themselves; Babel was to be a statement that spoke of a greatness and power that would intimidate and awe those who saw it.

Monument building was not unique to Babel; most ancient civilizations (and some modern ones) emphasized monument-building as a representation of power, wealth, and greatness. God, of course, confounded the language of the builders of Babel and men moved away from its ruins, not in repentance, but in defeat.

To the Christian, Babel represents man's ongoing rebellion against God, a rebellion repeated many times in history. Fallen man is running away from God and still believes that he can not only determine good and evil for himself, but build cities, institutions, and entire cultures in terms of it. To "be as gods," to rival heaven, is still the dream of fallen man. Babel is still the dream of any who would make a nation, a regime, or culture the ultimate unity and manifestation of power and greatness. Man has repeatedly tried to create new Babels whenever he has sought an ascendant unity and power outside of God. Only the methods have changed. The monuments men build now are made of philosophy, science, law, education, technology, and politics. Of these they build towers with which they seek to rival heaven and reign as gods over all things under them.

In this work, my father traces some of these arrogant trends of modern thought since the Enlightenment's conscious return to Greek humanism, which was its reaction to the theocentric thought of the Protestant Reformation. He begins with a chapter on the Marquis de Sade, whom he viewed as a self-consciously consistent rebel against God, and hence a forerunner of modern thought. Sade was more than just history's most infamous sexual pervert. He was an intelligent man who took humanism to its logical conclusion. Sade saw man as the infallible moral authority. He was a homosexual who favored abortion as a means of population control, infanticide, theft, incest, sodomy, and murder. Sade defended as legitimate anything man could conceive. Sade saw Christianity as incompatible with man's authority and sought its abolition. He was so consistent that he spent much of his time in prison; his perversity swayed few.

After the Enlightenment, while the West still thought and acted in the context of Christianity, others sought a more intellectual method of eliminating Christianity. They did so by destroying the authority of Christianity by reducing it to one option among many. Once Christianity's claim to transcendent authority was destroyed, hostility to the faith could use the banner of freedom and democracy. The method by which Christianity was made one option, and in fact an illegitimate option, was by making nature primary, nature the norm (i.e., good). If nature was good, then that which is not natural (i.e., supernatural), such as Christianity, was illegitimate.

The Enlightenment needed naturalism as a basis for its radical humanism. That is why the intellectual world after the Enlightenment so eagerly welcomed the ideas of Charles Darwin. Darwin gave a naturalistic scientific rationale for the Enlightenment's naturalism. If nature is the source of all, it is the source of ethics, morality, law, and all else previously explained in terms of transcendent moral law. The supernatural was then defined as unscientific, and an illegitimate imposition on nature. Modern man had engineered naturalism as the foundation of his new Babel.

Genesis shows us that the natural world was cursed as part of man's fall, that there is no independent "nature," only the natural, now cursed, creation of God. Looking to nature as a norm is embracing the world of the Fall. It is also to claim Satan's promise that man can be his own god, because "nature" does not speak, it is interpreted by man who sees the world in terms of his faith.

By accepting the fallen realm of nature as normative, man accepts his own fallen nature as normative. Fallen man sees the fallen creation (and himself as part of it) and, playing god, declares, "It is good. Sin is normal. Sin is good." Once the premise of naturalism works its way through man's thinking, the only real evil is the claim of transcendent moral law. That which is natural is the norm, and is good. That is the basis of the *Playboy* philosophy and the modern justification for prostitution and all other forms of sexual promiscuity. By a consistent naturalistic argument, all moral ethic and law is arbitrary and subjective, for all that man does or imagines becomes natural. This is why my father saw the Marquis de Sade as the first self-consciously modern man. This book is about how modern man is catching up with his conclusions and his ethical anarchism.

In proclaiming the Gospel of the Kingdom of God, the modern Christian must confront the Kingdom of Satan and its proclamation of man's ethical autonomy in terms of naturalism. Too frequently we react to some new perversity by declaring, "It's not natural" or "It's abnormal." In so arguing we have lost the battle, for we are speaking in terms of naturalism. Christianity must confront man's desire to be as god with the living God, and man's naturalistic philosophy with God's transcendent Word. Moral issues must be met with moral absolutes, though fallen man needs grace for those absolutes to result in repentance and faith.

Christianity created a Western civilization based on Christian thought and Biblical law. It was far from perfect, but its foundation was so sure, that men are still desperately attempting to undo its progress. De Sade saw the future which is now before us: freedom from God as a moral absolute. We have gone from the Enlightenment's elevation of man's reason to nihilism, from a denial of God to a denial of meaning, and from a contempt for Biblical morality to a love of evil: "All they that hate me love death" (Proverbs 8:36).

Much of modern thought came through the Romantics and was absorbed into our culture as a harmless literary trend. The Romantics saw virtue as absolute freedom from constraint and vice as repressed desire. Man's problem according to the Romantics was bondage to God, not bondage to sin. They popularized contempt for moral humanity, God, and family while positioning themselves as social prophets and victims of the ignorant and bigoted masses.

Karl Marx introduced a new element. He was less interested in ideas than in action. What made his scientific socialism "scientific" was that it was artificial, man made, and hence non-moral. It was a blueprint for forcing change.

Through Charles Darwin gave naturalism its own science, he also shifted its direction. The Enlightenment looked to nature and reason as the source of truth, yet Darwin destroyed this conception of nature by making it the realm of random chance. After Darwin, truth and ethics were both arbitrary. Not only was mindless, arbitrary violence certain, but so too its defense. Modern man is transforming his entire culture in terms of Darwin's naturalistic, evolutionary presupposition. Man is becoming what he professes to be, an amoral animal.

This regression of man and his culture is what Cornelius Van Til described as "integration into the void."

The modern thinkers and ideas represented in this book are not all in agreement; rebels run from God in different directions. Revolution against God's moral order has no order itself except in terms of its common antagonism to God. Men cannot be gods; all they can do is rebel against the true God. They define themselves by negation, by rebellion, by challenging God. They call evil good and good evil and pride themselves on intellectual achievement. Post-Enlightenment humanism's optimism ended with the horrors of World War I, though it revived briefly with the cult of science after the mid-Twentieth Century. It seems now to be burning out. In the last century it was furthered not by poets and literature, but by revolution, genocide, and military and statist force.

The dream of Babel is all around us; it is part of man's rebellion against God. Man wants to challenge heaven, to rival it, and to institutionalize his rebellion so that others are awed and intimidated. Much of my father's ministry was teaching people about the particulars of applying the faith with a view to seeing the big picture — seeing the scope of man's sin juxtaposed with Christ's regeneration and ultimate victory over all sin. The point of this book is that men must stand for the antithesis of modern naturalistic thought, for life in God rather than the love of death.

The point of the account of Babel was that men must remember that God sees man's sin and that He will confound it. Still, man has built many Babels since Genesis 11 and continues to do so.

Non-Christian man seeks to move towards a sadistic culture. Christian man, my father believed, must move in terms of the reconstruction of all things in terms of the supernatural God and His Word. Though we must challenge evil, we do not do so in terms of the modern lawless man. We challenge evil with righteousness. We present natural man with supernatural man, Jesus Christ. Reconstruction cannot be forced on a culture. It begins with natural man having been born again as a new creation in Christ Jesus and the rethinking of all things in terms of the supernatural Word of God. Reconstruction is about learning how to be citizens of the Kingdom of God. This book will help keep you from being its traitors, or collaborators with the Kingdom of Satan.

In examining the evil, anti-God rebellion that much modern thought represents, we must limit our pessimism to natural man and remain hopeful in the promises of God. Christ told us He has overcome the world. The evil we see is naturalistic man in his death throes, the confusion of a Babel. God's Word and His Savior sit exalted in heaven. The future is certain. God's way is the way of life, grace, mercy, and blessing. This is the certainty of our hope and the power of our message to a fallen world racing towards the logical outcome of its rebellion, death.

Mark R. Rushdoony
Vallecito, California
June 5, 2003

Chapter 1

The Marquis de Sade

Gnosticism was an indirect attack on Christianity and God's sovereignty. This indirectness did not diminish in the least its very real enmity. The pattern of Gnostic groups from the beginning has been to present themselves as the true interpreters of the hidden meaning of Christianity. Thus, while radically at odds with orthodox Christianity, the Gnostic cults have normally claimed to adhere to it and to "reveal" its true meaning. There was nothing indirect about the Marquis de Sade: his attack on Christianity was as direct as possible.

The Enlightenment, a European movement, began in England in the time of Charles II, 1660 on. Its roots, however, were deep in the medieval centuries. The Enlightenment shifted the center of interest from God to man, and from the Church to the State, except in the German states, where the university gained centrality. The intellectuals, the self–styled "men of reason," saw themselves as the prophets of the new order of the ages. In time, too, the performing arts replaced the mass and the church service. Man was now the measure of all things, and it was man's will that needed to be done. With man in charge, progress was held to be inevitable, and it was only a question of time before a utopia would be achieved.

Enlightenment humanism began with the "moral baggage" of its context, Christendom, but, *in practice*, it steadily stripped off all morality in favor of self-enjoyment. At the same time, being at war with God, *profanation* became a prized pleasure.

John Wilmot, Earl of Rochester (1647-1680), was a profligate who, in denying God, denied the possibility of humanity becoming moral and truly honest:

> Thus here you see what Human Nature craves,
> Most men are Cowards, all Men shou'd be Knaves.
> The Difference lies, as far as I can see,
> Not in the Thing itself, but the Degree;
> And all the subject Matter of Debate,
> Is only who's a Knave of the First Rate.[1]

Humanism begins by affirming the natural goodness of all men as against the Biblical doctrines of the fall and man's depravity. It affirms the sovereignty of goodness, truth, and beauty, and their prevalence and pre-eminence among men. Before long it despises these things in favor of their reverse. Gaining sexual license, instead of enjoying sex, held to be beautiful and good at first, is polluted in as many ways as possible.

The Restoration poet, John Callop (1632/3?-1676 or after?) was extravagant in his praise of both Charles I, and Charles II, whom he claimed was greater than Charlemagne, holding, in Conrad Hilberry's words, Charles II to be "a very Christ, appearing in his thirtieth year to reform England."[2] This is in line with Callop's part in a baroque genre in praise of an ugly or a deformed mistress. Callop praised women, aging and in decay, with bad teeth, a bowed back, over-weight, and so on.

---

1. "A Satyr Against Mankind," in John Wilmot, Earl of Rochester, *A Satire Against Mankind and Other Poems*, edited by Harry Levin (Norfold, Connecticut: New Directions, 1942).
2. Conrad Hilberry, editor, *The Poems of John Callop* (Madison, Wisconsin: University of Wisconsin Press, 1962), 9.

The contempt for beauty meant the praise of its opposites.[3] For Callop, as for Thomas Hobbes, "political power is a matter of force, not right."[4] For him, "The greatest injury is the greatest right" because it is clearly triumphant.[5]

Clearly, the moral universe was being turned upside down. The courts of Europe, from 1660 to 1800 practiced this new way of life. More than a few scholars have pointed out that such courtly practices far exceeded Sade's own acts. Of course, Sade spent so much of his life in prison that his sexual activity was accordingly restricted! The pleasure in sin was a passion of the times; in Sade, it was an obsession. Moreover, Sade was at all times and in all things in total war against God. The dominating motive of Sade's life was his war against God. Because the Bible told him that man is made in God's image, Sade had to do everything to defame and deface that image in his intense hatred of God. As Simone de Beauvoir pointed out, Sade openly acknowledged his coprophilia.[6] The action in Sade's writings is always anti-God and, then, anti-man. It was as a student that I learned from my reading what was later confirmed to me by a few who dealt with mental patients, namely, that the hatred of God is so intense with some that they eat feces to defile God's image in them. Their hatred of God is personal, physical, and violent. Sade chose Easter day to whip Rose Keller. His life and his writings were an unceasing act of war against God. Beauvoir saw Sade's hatred against God and His creation, and she cited these words of Sade:

> Ah, how many times, by God, have I not longed to be able to assail the sun, snatch it out of the universe, make a general darkness, or use that star to burn the world! Oh, that would be a crime.[7]

---

3. *Ibid.*, 19ff.
4. *Ibid.*, 10.
5. *Ibid.*, 75.
6. Simone de Beauvoir, "Must We Burn Sade?" in *The Marquis de Sade: The 120 Days of Sodom, and other writings* (New York, N.Y.: Grove Press, 1966), 25.
7. *Ibid.*, 32.

Above all, Sade's enemy was God. "The idea of God is the sole wrong for which I cannot forgive mankind."[8] Like Camus after him, Sade chose evil because God is good. He chose filth, corruption, horror, and villany because they were the antithesis of the good and the holy.[9] Sade willed the death of God for himself. He saw, not a universal harmony of interests, but a cosmic conflict of interests. "My neighbor is nothing to me; there is not the slightest relationship between him and myself."[10] Sade was also always marked by *a will to death*. He wrote, "The principle of life in all beings is no other than the death principle."[11] According to Richard Seaver and Austryn Wainhouse, "Sade sought condemnation."[12] More honestly stated, we would have to say that Sade sought hell. For him, man is depraved, and the human race should be allowed to die out.[13] Sade held that all things work together for evil.[14] He hated fertility, advocated birth control,[15] and wanted, as we have seen, universal death. Pleasure, he held, must be solitary, and there is joy in oppressing others.[16] The world, Sade held, is over-populated, or, at least, France was.[17] He was against all laws restricting the freedom to do evil. Each women "must belong to all who claim her."[18] Marriage had to be destroyed.[19] Perversions were urged as a prevention of births.[20] For Sade, man's heart, being totally evil, was the infallible moral authority.[21] Sade, a homosexual, favored abortion and

---

8. *Ibid.*, 41.
9. *Ibid.*, 43n.
10. *Ibid.*, 58.
11. Pierre Klossowski, "Nature as Destructive Principle," in *ibid.*, 78.
12. Richard Seaver and Austryn Wainhouse, compilers, translators, *The Marquis de Sade, the complete Justine, Philosophy in the Bedroom, and other writings*, "Foreword" (New York, N.Y.: Grove Press, 1965), xi.
13. "Eugenie de Franval," *Ibid.*, 388.
14. "Justine," in *ibid.*, 481f.
15. *Ibid.*, 586.
16. *Ibid.*, 603ff., 645f.
17. "Philosophy in the Bedroom," *ibid.*, 216.
18. *Ibid.*, 219.
19. *Ibid.*, 222.
20. *Ibid.*, 229f.
21. *Ibid.*, 236.

infanticide.[22] Cruelty was for him a consummate form of pleasure.[23] He referred to Satan as the "one and unique god of my soul."[24]

Sade set forth his thinking perhaps most clearly in a pamphlet inserted into his "Philosophy in the Bedroom." Its title, "Yet Another Effort, Frenchmen, If You Would Become Republicans," calls for a great effort to complete the French Revolution. Christianity must be eliminated and theft, incest, sodomy, and murder tolerated. As Lynn Hunt pointed out, for Edmund Burke, in *Reflections on the Revolution in France* (1790), this was a logical conclusion to "this new conquering empire of light and reason."[25]

Because Sade was so *consistently* evil, he was more logical than most evil men and most churchmen, whose *inconsistent* profession of Christianity blurs their vision badly. Sade's fundamental premise in "Yet Another Effort, Frenchmen,..." was simply this: having abandoned Christianity, men should therefore logically abandon all law: "for what should we, who have no religion, do with law?"[26] Law being the will of the sovereign, to abandon God as sovereign means to abandon His law. And, if man is now sovereign, how can there be any law over man? Is not man's will the *only* law? The French Revolution, Sade hoped, had also dethroned Caesar and should abandon the State: "annihilate forever what may one day destroy your work."[27] Men should follow "Nature, equally dictating vices and virtues to us."[28] Equality, he told the revolutionists, is "that foremost law of your new government."[29] The morality of love for one's neighbor was for Sade, absurd. Sade opposed capital punishment, and laws

---

22. *Ibid.*, 249.
23. *Ibid.*, 252ff.
24. *Ibid.*, 272.
25. Lynn Hunt, *The Family Romance of the French Revolution* (Berkeley, California: University of California Press, 1992), 139.
26. Sade, in *The Complete Justine, etc.*, 296.
27. *Ibid.*, 297.
28. *Ibid.*, 307.
29. *Ibid.*, 309.

against murder.[30] The only proper morality for a republican government was its self-perpetuation.[31] One can add that it was to exist to prevent the existence of Christianity and its laws: republican manners required immorality to demonstrate equality. All women should be the property of all men: there should be *no exclusiveness* in any sphere of life.[32] He held that he had the right of possession over any woman, and "I have incontestable rights to the enjoyment of her; I have the right to force from her this enjoyment, if she refuse me it for whatever the cause may be."[33] This should be true of females from their early years. Sade favored incest: he wanted it made into law,[34] and also sodomy. Savages are closest to Nature and the most ferocious, as all should be, Sade believed. Child-killing to avoid "over-population" he also favored.[35]

According to Simone de Beauvoir, sodomy was central to Sade's thinking: "There is no perversion of which he speaks so often and with so much satisfaction, and even impassioned vehemence."[36] There is no evidence, she wrote, that Sade ever engaged in normal sexuality.[37] Max Stirner in his, *The Ego and His Own*, clearly followed Sade in his views of God, law, and morality. A Sadean man of wimpish traits in the Twentieth Century was Salvador Dali, the artist.[38]

Sadean thinking has been an underground movement in history since his time, perhaps in part because of Sade's counsel in *Juliette*:

> True wisdom, my dear Juliette, does not consist in repressing our vices, because since these vices constitute almost the only happiness in our life to wish to repress them would be to become our own executioners. But it

---

30. *Ibid.*, 310.
31. *Ibid.*, 315.
32. *Ibid.*, 318ff.
33. *Ibid.*, 320.
34. *Ibid.*, 324.
35. *Ibid.*, 336.
36. Simone de Beauvoir, in Sade, *120 Days of Sodom*, etc., 23.
37. *Ibid.*, 24.
38. Tim McGirk, *Wicked Lady: Salvador Dali's Muse* (London, England: Hutchinson, 1989).

> consists in abandoning ourselves to them with such secrecy, and such extensiveness that we may never be caught out. Do not be afraid that this may diminish their delight: mystery adds to the pleasure. Moreover, such behaviour ensures impunity, and is not impunity the most delicious nourishment of debauchery?[39]

The world of Sade is all around us. It colors our media, television, and the films. It is an undercurrent in modern life. It appears, for example, in the coprophiliac plus activities of a prominent "rock star."[40] It is present everywhere in what Gallagher has aptly termed our pornographic culture, in which sex is separated from the family and procreation and reduced to irresponsible pleasure. Modern sexual repression bars honest treatments of sexuality and has made sexual androgyny "the dominant cultural message."[41]

Lynn Hunt's book gives us much evidence about our revolution: prior to the French Revolution, the family provided the pattern for society. Rulers were the fathers of their countries. Parental respect was given to all authorities, and the professed goal of society was to be bound together as a family. Though often abused, this ideal had, over the centuries, also provided nations with a cohesive premise.

The French Revolution was preceded by a pornographic assault on the monarchy. It concentrated at first on the queen, Marie Antoinette, and then on King Louis XVII. Books with pornographic illustrations abounded. The premise of the revolutionary writers was not, respect authority, but, like the logo on a T-shirt I saw not too long ago, "Fuck Authority." Basic to the French Revolution, according to Lynn Hunt, was "the underlying interconnections between pornography and politics."[42]

---

39. Leonard de Saint-Yves, editor, translator, *Selected Writings of De Sade* (New York, N.Y.: British Book Centre, 1954), 215f.
40. Mike Sager, "Sex and Drugs and Rock 'N' Roll Especially Sex," in *Spy*, vol. 7, February, 1993, 58-63.
41. Maggie Gallagher, *Enemies of Eros* (Chicago, Illinois: Bonus Books, 1989), 3ff., 81f., 251ff., 264.
42. *Ibid.*, 91.

We miss the meaning of much of the Twentieth Century if we neglect the relationship between the "hard" and "soft" pornography of our time and the spirit of revolution. Its premise is also that of the Marquis de Sade: abolish God and law, reduce all things to equality, and man will then be free to enjoy himself.

Against all this, an antinomian church is helpless. Those who, while professing to believe the Bible, are antinomian, have already yielded the essentials: a God who is not sovereign and therefore not the source of law is hardly God at all! The Modernists *openly* surrender the Biblical doctrine of God and God's law, so they begin in Sade's camp.

Should we be surprised that antinomian pastors and priests are so much involved in homosexuality, child molestation, and adultery, and often have a taste for pornography?

Some years ago, when Knud Rasmussen asked an Iglulik Inuit "wise man" what his people believed, he was told, "What do we believe? We don't believe, we only fear."[43] We have today two groups in the Twentieth Century world: those who only fear, and those who live only to enjoy their Sadean desires. There is no future for either of them. We need to say with the psalmist, "It is time for thee, LORD, to work: for they have made void thy law" (Ps. 119:126). Moreover, we need to take our stand with the triumphant men of old who said, "I shall not die, but live, and declare the works of the LORD" (Ps. 118:17).

---

43. Robert B. Edgerton, *Sick Societies, Challenging the Myth of Primitive Harmony* (New York, N.Y.: Macmillan, 1992), 128.

Chapter 2

Supernatural vs. Natural Man

One of the quiet goals of the Enlightenment was the disestablishment of churches and of Christianity. By its enthronement of Nature and of natural law, it worked to supplant Christianity and God's law. In time, of course, natural law gave way to statist law; the state was seen by Hegel as Nature's supreme expression.

A *first* step in this process of disestablishment was to reduce Christianity to an *option* for man, a matter of choice, not of necessity. *The realm of necessity* was held to be civil government. Freedom came to mean deliverance from the Church to the State, from supernatural mandates and laws to 'natural' and statist laws. The Reformation had said plainly that Biblical faith requires belief in God's *predestination,* in *God's sovereign choice*, whether or not men are elect or non-elect. This was reversed by the Enlightenment, and then by Arminianism. *Sovereign choice was transferred to man.* Man, it was held, has the option to choose God or to reject Him, to declare God to be elect or non-elect.

Second, a logical consequence of this position was for man to reject the triune God and Christianity and to *ban* this faith as 'inimical' to man and to a free democratic, or republican, society. This step the French Revolution, and especially the Marquis de Sade, took boldly. Christianity holds this world to be a *created* order and therefore totally dependent upon the triune God. John 1:3 says of God the Word, "All things were made by Him; and without Him was not anything made that was made." This *absolute dependency* is of the world upon God, not upon the Church. After Darwin especially, this dependency was denied, and instead men and the world order were seen as rather dependent on the State. Especially since World War II, there has been a steady growth of hostility to God and Christianity in the name of freedom. If the natural order is determinative, then any supernatural law or mandate is an infringement on human freedom. A ban on God's law is therefore sought.

The issue is between supernatural man and natural man, between Jesus Christ and His new humanity, and the fallen Adam and his unregenerate humanity.

In 1938, Eugen Rosenstock-Huessy's *Out of Revolution, the Autobiography of Western Man,* was published. It was, in effect, an account of the great counter-revolution of the natural man against the supernatural man, Jesus Christ and His new humanity. The Luther of this counter-revolution was a fictional character, Faust, in particular Goethe's Faust.[1] Men sought a re-migration from Israel to Nature, from a covenanted people to a natural one. They sought in effect an ark to take them back, unlike Noah, to the world *before* the Flood, to a world where men lived very long lives in contempt of God. "Natural law bore the proud name of a Sacrament."[2] In the world of the Enlightenment, "The princes took over the functions of the popes, the successors of Peter."[3]

In this world of the natural man, the Bible is anathema. The state school textbook for sex education, *Changing Bodies, Changing Lives,* says in its opening pages, "There isn't any rule

1. Eugen Rosenstock-Huessy *Out of Revolution* (New York, N.Y.: William Morrow, 1938), 433ff.
2. *Ibid.*, 680-683.
3. *Ibid.*, 401.

book... There's no 'right' way or 'right' age to have life experiences."[4] There can, in this perspective, be no right nor wrong because there can be no rule book, no Bible. Whatever is good is natural and therefore good. Evil is the anti-natural and therefore supernatural or Christian. Hitler is seen as evil simply by associating him with Christianity, even though he was an atheist, anti-Christian, and a nationalistic Marxist. The premise in school sex education classes is that there are no 'right' or 'wrong' answers, "just *your* answers." The textbook, *Learning About Sex*, states:

> I cannot judge the "rightness" or "wrongness" of any of these behaviours. Instead, I hope that you can find the sexual life-style which is best for your life.[5]

Not surprisingly, many educators work to bar any teaching on Biblical morality. Chastity is often a forbidden subject because it represents the standards of supernatural man. Before sex education spread through state schools in the 1970s, teenage pregnancy had been declining over a period of more than a dozen years in the study, but it rose sharply with the introduction of sex education classes.[6] Since the goal of such teaching was, and is, to further the triumph of natural man, it must be said that the results are *desired* results.

As against the Biblical view that humanity outside of Christ is fallen, totally depraved, and in sin, the humanists assert the natural goodness, or, at least, moral neutrality of the natural man. Carl Rogers, very influential in these educational circles that enthrone the natural man, has held that, necessary to sound education, is "a profound trust in the human organism."[7] *Values clarification* teaching works to deliver the child from Biblical laws into a totally personal and relativistic "morality." As one teacher at least has insisted, "Is it right *for you*?" No moral arbiter exists beyond the natural man. As a

---

4. Thomas Sowell, *Inside American Education* (New York, N.Y., The Free Press of Macmillan, 1993), 4ff.
5. *Ibid.*, 53.
6. *Ibid.*, 63.
7. *Ibid.*, 56.

result, fornication, adultery, homosexuality, and other lawless practices are affirmed to be natural and are promoted. Christian standards are derided and peer values are stressed.[8] Such teachings are, as Sowell noted, "pretentious mush,"[9] but they are still poisonous in their pretentions.

Their implicit goal is anarchy. If every man's values are valid in the sphere of sexual morality, why not follow Sade's logic in the spheres of theft and murder? Karl Marx rightly feared the logic of Max Stirner. Stirner saw that, given the truth of atheism, there could be no law governing man in any sphere. Every man would be his own law. The key sentence in *Judges*, repeated more than once, is, "In those days there was no king in Israel: every man did that which was right in his own eyes" (Judges 21:25). Having rejected God as their King and Lawgiver, every man was his own god, king, and law.

Margaret Mead, who was hardly a friend of God, and not at all favorable to a Biblical faith, still observed, in a book very antithetical to Christianity,

> The question of morality, of the public observance of declared standards of tolerable and intolerable forms of petty corruption, of the interaction between different systems of morality, loyalty, and rake-off, present an acute problem to our interdependent world in many ways. Social life is based on the trustworthiness of others in the same system.[10]

She saw the need for some common ground, but she sought it in man, in "the trustworthiness of others in the same system."

This trustworthiness has been singularly lacking. It has been abundantly evident, especially since World War II and the decline of attention to Biblical law, that men and nations are not trustworthy. What sanctions, then, can the nations provide against "intolerable" actions on the part of men and nations? The United Nations has been the answer, and

---

8. *Ibid.*, 54.
9. *Ibid.*, 62.
10. Margaret Mead, *World Enough, Rethinking the Future* (Boston, Massachusetts: Little Brown,1975), 153f.

military coercion. But in terms of what moral standard? Repeated evils have been routinely overlooked, while action has been taken in other cases on political grounds. The United Nations has not advanced morality because it has none. Its existence, moreover, is a contradiction. If the natural man is normative, then why should there be nation-states or a world state? The earlier anarchists were logical: if Nature is normative, and man is naturally good, then the State is an obstruction to a free, happy, and prosperous social order.

Indeed, for these anarchists, there were and are two impediments to the free and happy society. *First*, of course, there is Christianity with its insistence on supernatural man and its negative view of natural man. The freedom of man, it was held, requires the elimination of Christianity. *Second*, there is the state. Because it introduces coercion into human action, it prevents freedom and therefore is an enemy of natural man.

The anarchists, however, lacked the honesty of the Marquis de Sade because they assumed the natural goodness of man. They gave man a *moral* nature, and, in this respect, they were still in the fold of Christianity because they assumed that men have a *moral* nature. The concept of natural man, however, requires that we believe, with Nietzsche that man must awaken to the fact that God is dead, and we must live beyond good and evil. Earlier, the Marquis de Sade had vindicated every crime conceivable as valid because it occurred in Nature. Nothing therefore could be condemned without giving assent to the standards of supernatural man. To condemn *anything* in the world of Nature as evil is, logically, a heresy for humanism. It is like saying that some aspect of the Biblical God is evil! It leads to a radical collapse of whatever faith it is that adopts such a position.

It has been often pointed out that the Marquis de Sade did not practice as many perversions as were routine among the aristocracy of his day. Of course, he was in prison too much of his life to be able to do so! In his writings, however, he was insistently logical in stating that to believe in natural man means to accept all practices other than those governed by the supernatural God and His word as *acceptable.* No ground exists for natural man to condemn any natural human act on extraneous grounds. Every natural act is its own justification. No standard outside of the act is permissible. Max Stirner agreed with this. He wrote, in *The Ego and His Own*,

> Take notice how a "moral man" behaves, who today often thinks he is through with God and throws off Christianity as a bygone thing. If you ask him whether he has ever doubted that the copulation of brother and sister is incest, that monogamy is the truth of marriage, that filial piety is a sacred duty, etc., then a moral shudder will come over him at the conception of one being allowed to touch his sister as wife also, etc. And whence this shudder? Because *he believes* in those moral commandments. This moral *faith* is deeply rooted in his breast. Much as he rages against the *pious* Christians, he himself has nevertheless as thoroughly remained a Christian — to wit, a *moral* Christian. In the form of morality Christianity holds him a prisoner, and a prisoner under *faith.* Monogamy is to be something sacred, and he who may live in bigamy is punished as a *criminal*; he who commits incest suffers as a *criminal.* Those who are always crying that religion is not to be regarded in the State, and the Jew is to be a citizen equally with the Christian, show themselves in accord with this. Is not this incest and monogamy a *dogma of faith*? Touch it, and you will learn by experience how this moral man is a *hero* of faith too, not less than Krummacher, not less than Philip II. These fight for the faith of the Church, he for the faith of the State, or the moral laws of the State; for articles of faith, both condemn him who acts otherwise than *their faith* will allow. The brand of "crime" is stamped upon him, and he may languish in reformatories, in jails. Moral faith is as fanatical as religious faith! They call that "liberty of faith" then, when brother and sister, on account of a relation that they should have settled with their "conscience," are thrown into prison. "But they set a pernicious example." Yes, indeed others might have taken the notion that the State had no business to meddle with their relation, and thereupon "purity of morals" would go to ruin. So then the

religious heroes of faith are zealous for the "sacred God," the moral ones for the "sacred good."[11]

If we understand what Stirner held, then we can grasp the direction and meaning of sex education in our state schools, of the arguments used by homosexuals in demanding their version of life, and we can understand why more and more judges are delivering decisions after the manner of Sade.

A homosexual San Francisco, California supervisor has declared, "This campaign is a spiritual war."[12] If we establish society on the premises of natural man, then it follows, as the California Court of Appeals held in 1991, that sodomy is a constitutional right. The State Supreme Court held the issue to be unresolved until the scope of "the right to privacy" could be determined.[13] However, given the prevailing premise of the priority of the natural man, if not the exclusivism of the natural, the homosexual faith will prevail *unless* the priority of the supernatural man, Jesus Christ, and His law word are re-established and extended.

---

11. Max Stirner, *The Ego and His Own* (New York, N.Y.: The Modern Library, n. d.), 47f. Stirner, whose real name was Kaspar Schmidt, held that "All things are nothing to me," because "Nothing is more to me than myself." His dates were 1805-1856.

12. Chuck and Donna McIlhenny with Frank York, *When the Wicked Seize a City* (Lafayette, Indiana: Huntington House, 1993), 197.

13. *Ibid.*, 225.

Chapter 3

Sadean Man as God

The world of the Marquis de Sade is all around us. It is so powerful that a monthly such as *The World and I* (October, 1993) devoted forty-six pages to the analysis of "Homosexuality: New Virtue or Old Vice?" The editor, left unnamed, confronted the issue realistically, declaring,

> The great social barrier to homosexuality is the family. As long as the family, as now understood, commands the rational and emotional assent of most people, it is hard for homosexuality to enter the mainstream of American life.[1]

Until now, the family has been the basis of civilizations. The editor considers the question of whether or not the family is ultimately biological or social, recognizes both elements, and sees its historical development as basically social. The religious, the *Biblical*, character of the family is by-passed. This is to confuse the issue. The Hebrew and Christian families have seen theirs as a God-ordained order, and homosexuality as the *antithesis* of this and therefore punishable by death (Lev. 18:22; 20:13; Deut. 23:17; 1 Kings 14:24; Romans 1:24-32; etc.)

---

1. Introduction, "Homosexuality: New Virtue or Old Vice?" in *The World and I,* October, 1993, 361.

However, thorough analysis of this question is inadequate as long as we by-pass the religious question. The Bible sees homosexuality as an offense against God's fundamental order and as the *burning out* of man. The translation in Romans 1:27, *burned* is literally *burned out.* The violation of the image of God in man is so great in male and female homosexuality that it is their *burning out.*

The editor sees the *first* or primary function of the family as biological, to produce children and "to raise" (or, rear) them. If science realizes the dream of Aldous Huxley's *Brave New World* to produce babies in a test tube, will that eliminate the family? A biological or a social function can be altered almost to the point of elimination, but not so a religious one. The editor is not hostile to the religious, but he is somewhat indifferent to it. He sees, however, as a *given*, that homosexuals "have the rights of any citizen."[2] This means a failure to recognize the radical hostility between orthodox Biblical faith and homosexuals.

Thomas J. Ward and Frederick A. Swarts write on "The Mainstreaming of Homosexuality."[3] Their main thesis is that it has not been shown that homosexuality is either genetic or immutable. More scientific research is necessary before changes in social policy are made. Their reliance is thus on scientific research rather than religious and moral absolutes. After all, if we believe in an evolutionary perspective, the scientific facts can change. We can add that, precisely because we have looked to scientific answers, we are in the crisis that exists. God's word is unchanging. The stance of psychiatrists was changed by means of pressure tactics.

Even more now, politics is at work. Both Republicans and Democrats responded to homosexual pressures, and President Clinton has championed their cause. More than a usual number of male and female homosexuals "glorify" his administration. Government, media, and businesses are

---

2. *Ibid.*, 363.

3. Thomas J. Ward and Frederick A. Swarts, "The Mainstreaming of Homosexuality," in *Ibid.*, 365-381.

cooperative with homosexuals, and the mainline churches, in varying degrees, are also receptive. Of course, the pressure (and the threats) are substantial.[4] School books are more openly anti-Christian and pro-homosexual. Toleration and acceptance of homosexuality and other deviant practices is now a part of statist education.

One aspect of the war against Christian premises is the argument from science. Some have insisted on a genetic basis for homosexuality; others maintain that it is a matter of choice and is a choice as valid as any other in a value-free world. The "scientific" studies are suspect, as are the various pro-homosexual scholars who continue to use the clearly invalid figures of the Kinsey Report. What is clear is that, even *before* AIDS, homosexuals had a poor life expectancy. Also, the *legal* acceptance of homosexuality has opened the door to demands for the legalization of a variety of other practices, such as pedophilia, bestiality, and incest.

The perspective of Ward and Swarts is obviously not Biblical. They see the past treatment of homosexuals as "cold, insensitive," and they believe that they should be treated "in a responsible, compassionate manner."[5] Should we treat rapists and murderers with compassion also? Is this an issue for *compassion* or for *justice*? If they are *at the least* a health problem in the population, is it insensitive or unjust to recognize this? If they are a factor in the sexual abuse of the young, is it unjust to analyze and deal with that fact? And what about compassion towards the many young victims of homosexuals?

Ward and Swarts recognize that homosexuals are demanding "much more than respect and tolerance." Is the answer to this demand that we accept the normality of homosexuality "the exploring (of) the scientific validity thereof?" Do religion and morality have nothing to do with the matter? Is not this pseudo-neutralism as wrong as homosexuality?

---

4. See Chuck and Donna McIlhenny with Frank York, *When the Wicked Seize a City* (Lafayette, Louisiana: Huntington House, 1993).

5. Ward and Swarts in *The World and I*, 381.

The World and I gives no space to the Biblical position, but it does give twelve pages to Franklin E. Kameny, a "gay activist," writing on "Deconstructing the Traditional Family." Kameny has served on the District of Columbia Commission on Human Rights, and on the board of the District of Columbia American Civil Liberties Union.

Kameny's belief is in freedom in moral matters, which he sees as basic to the First Amendment. He insists that the burden of proof in limiting any kind of sexual activity rests with those who seek such limitations. But if no religious or moral grounds are acceptable, how can such proof be forthcoming? By definition, a Biblical standard is excluded.

Kameny begins by questioning the validity of the Biblical doctrine of the family, although he does not discuss the Bible. He insists on "the priority of the individual." But if the individual is prior to God or society, how can there be *any* law? He states,

> Society is a cultural artifact that has no legitimacy in its own right and no "rights" to which the interest of the individual need properly be subordinated. Illustratively, let the reader ask and answer why does society exist at all? Or, for what purpose does society exist? Or (a little less neutrally), what excuse does society have for existing? The answer is, of course, that society exists solely to enable its members, as individuals, to lead better and more rewarding, fulfilling, and satisfying lives (as they define those terms for themselves) than they could without the assistance of society. There is no other reason for having a society.[6]

In a debate with John Lofton, Kameny argued for the legitimacy of bestiality. Kameny believes that society exists for the same reason as automobiles do, "to serve our purposes." There is thus "no legitimate basis" for limiting the individual's freedom. "Above all, the First Amendment creates an inescapable moral relativism for our whole nation."[7] *No moral*

---

6. Franklin E. Kameny, "Deconstructing the Traditional Family," in *The World and I*, October, 1993, 384f.

7. Precis, *ibid.*, 385

code is thus tenable. He sees our society falsely guided by the "so-called Judeo-Christian religious precepts." This religious heritage cripples and binds our culture and the obsolete, outmoded standards should be discarded.[8]

> Thus the First Amendment creates an inescapable moral relativism, societal and cultural, for our nation taken as a whole. For example, I view homosexual sexual activity as not only not immoral, or sinful, or wrong, or undesirable, but as *affirmatively moral*, and virtuous, and right, and desirable. I take that as a moral absolute, and churches (Christian churches at that,) with which I have some association take the same view. I am not willing to concede that my moral absolutes are any less absolute than those of more orthodox religions that take an opposing view, nor need I in America.[9]

For Kameny, freedom is the moral absolute, which means that *anything goes.* In terms of his absolute, freedom, how can he limit it by stating that anything goes, provided that the other person is not hurt? How can that counter-standard be introduced? The goal of some is to lower the age of consent for children. Kinsey saw no harm in child molestation. Where are the limits? The individual and his freedom have no limits when made into an absolute. Kameny sees murder as an imposition on a non-consenting partner. Even then, he writes, "as a matter of philosophical principle, a government prohibiting murder needs, at some threshold point in the process, to have shouldered the burden of justification for its prohibition." On what grounds? Kameny does not say. For him, man has an "inalienable right" to be free to do as he pleases.[10] For Kameny, the freedom of the individual is radically uninhibited in theory. For him, this radical freedom "is what America is all about."[11]

---

8. *Ibid.* 387.
9. *Ibid.*, 389.
10. *Ibid.*, 390.
11. *Ibid.*, 395.

Editor Morton A. Kaplan tries "to apply some common sense to these issues," he says.[12] He avoids the religious foundation, of course. He recognizes that a "Kulturkampf" is in process, but he refuses to confront it religiously. As a result, we have a series of compromising statements. He wants to approve of the decriminalization of homosexual activities but not their full legitimation. Kaplan doubts that any "real expert" on the subject exists, but he will not consider a return to Biblical faith. As a result, he is unable to deal with Kameny's arguments.

Where does all this lead? The English *Weekly Telegraph*, issue no. 113, September 8-14, 1993, carried the obituary of Anne Cummings, writer and actress, and the authoress of erotic travelogues. Born on December 14, 1917, she died in 1993 at the age 75. She had been diagnosed HIV positive seven years previously. She had acted in films and had taught at the Michael Chekhov drama studio. She was the grand-daughter of a noted MP, was educated in schools in England and abroad, and had resided in England, Switzerland, South Africa, and the United States. She was described as a "sexual adventuress," and she wrote about her experiences.

> Cumming recalled a night in Paris where she stood on the street dressed only in a mink coat and fluffy slippers, baring her body to passing men. No one stopped.[13]

The same page of *The Weekly Telegraph* carries the obituary of the Anglican Bishop George Appleton, who, when he retired, said he was going to "prepare myself for the migration to the new order of being which cannot be far ahead."[14]

Ann Cumming and Bishop George Appleton belong to an older generation born with the trappings of civilization clinging to them. The new barbarians share their mindless perspective. They are relativists and Sadeans. No society, nor state, can long exist with such barbarians in its midst. Basic to

---

12. Morton A. Kaplan, "Common Sense on Gay Rights," in *ibid.*), 397.
13. "Ann Cumming," in *Weekly Telegraph*, issue. No 113, September 8-14, 1993, 38.
14. *Ibid.*, 38.

all their activity is an implicit and explicit belief that the will of the individual is the only law. No jungle is more deadly than the modern state and city. We see all around us the logic of man's fall, of Genesis 3:5, every man as his own god and law, doing that which is right in his own eyes (Judges 21:25).

Chapter 4

The War Against Morality and Communication

Our Lord tells us, "the children of this world are in their generation wiser than the children of light" (Luke 16:8). This is a sad fact and an important one. In one state, a lawsuit seeks to abolish any teaching of chastity from state schools as an establishment of religion. In Buffalo, New York, Paul C. Schenck, on a city school committee, found, as he said, "We can't mention God, but we can mention anal intercourse, oral sex, erections, and menstruation" in the public schools.[1]

The reason is an obvious one. Chastity is the imposition on the human order of a standard from the supernatural realm. In a purely naturalistic perspective, no norm from outside the natural realm is permissible, and hence an emphasis on virginity and chastity represent an imposition of a supernatural law upon man, i.e., an establishment of religion.

F.M. Christensen, a Canadian professor, has written on *Pornography, The Other Side*, a defense of pornography against all judgments against it. His argument has as its *first* and central principle the belief "that values must be based on needs."

---

[1]. Paul Schenck, with Robert L. Schenck, *The Extermination of Christianity, A Tyranny of Consensus* (Lafayette, Indiana: Huntington House, 1993), 26.

Whatever a man feels that he needs is thereby his value and is valid. The *second* major principle is equality; "each individual's well-being counts just as much as any other's." My needs are equally good as yours, and vice versa. *Third*, morality and immorality are relative to the individual's needs, and how they affect others.[2] In other words, man determines law and morality, and Christianity must be barred from *any* influence.

The *God is Dead Movement* of the early 1970s did *not* say that God is Himself dead but that He is dead to men; men no longer care whether He lives or not. This is our cultural position today. God must not be permitted to impinge on man's life because modern man has chosen to disregard Him and to live as though He were dead.

This is not a new perspective. When we go back to the early years of Christianity, and up to the fall of Rome, we find that the Mystery Religions arose and spread. Before that, Rome had been suspicious of these groups. In 186 B.C., the Roman historian Livy reported on a senate investigation of one such group. Their premise was a simple one: "To regard nothing as forbidden was among these people the summit of religious achievement."[3] The premise, which Rome regarded with dismay in 186 B.C., became in time the faith of many people, and Rome was therefore in the process of decay.

Christianity created a civilization based upon Christ's atonement and God's law. Since about 1850, the Christian premise of our civilization has been openly denied. Previously, there were many challenges, but this current one has come from scientists, scholars, educators, politicians, and churchmen. Its premise was at first humanism; it has since become nihilistic humanism. There is a war against any and all values and standards in all fields. Value and truth are now purely personal standards, unrelated to any reality outside or beyond man.

---

2. F.M. Christensen, *Pornography, The Other Side* (New York, N.Y., Praeger, 1990), 21f.
3. Marvin W. Meyer, editor, *The Ancient Mysteries, A Sourcebook* (San Francisco, California: Harper San Francisco, 1987), 86.

Dinesh D'Souza provides us with many examples of this in *Illiberal Education*:

> The Yale deconstructionist Geoffrey Hartman has complained about "the automatic valuing of works of art over works of commentary," and expressed his desire to lift criticism from its "second-class status in the world of letters."[4]

This means that Shakespeare and Milton are no better than their critics, and perhaps not as good. The deconstructionists "hold that literature is empty of meaning."[5] The critic supplies the meaning for the moment. This meaning need have no relation to historical reality. In terms of this, Maya Angelou, who had a part in the inauguration of President Clinton, has said, "I *know* that William Shakespeare was a black woman."[6]

We have a full-scale war against moral values, standards, and Biblical law and ethics. Universities have announced "a recruitment program offering preferential treatment for homosexuals and lesbians."[7] The Modern Language Association, once a clearly scholarly group, resolved, in 1987,

> Be it therefore resolved that the MLA will refrain from locating future conventions, not already scheduled, in any state that has criminalized acts of sodomy through legislation, unless that legislation, though still on the books, has been found to be unconstitutional, or the state has been enjoined from enforcing it through decisions rendered by the courts.[8]

This militant stand against Biblical law and morality is apparent in legislative and court actions. Max Stirner and Friedrich Nietzsche advocated the transvaluation of all life and morality, but this present generation has a sizeable element dedicated to living beyond good and evil. We have passed the

---

4. Dinesh D'Souza, *Illiberal Education* (New York, N.Y.: Vintage Books, Random House, 1991, 1992), 180.
5. *Ibid.*, 178.
6. *Ibid.*, from Maya Angelou, "Journey to the Heartland," Address to the National Assembly of Local Art Agencies," Cedar Rapids, Iowa, June 12, 1985), 157.
7. *Ibid.*, 5, 12.
8. *Ibid.*, 8.

point described by George Orwell about fifty years ago, when he observed, "We have now sunk to a depth where the restatement of the obvious is the first duty of intelligent men."[9] Such an attitude, John Lukaas held, means the end of the scientific world view.[10] Truth is gone, meaning is gone, and man is his own god and world. However, having denied *all* values, man can no longer maintain that he himself has any value. All man's pouting and shouting cannot obscure the fact that in a world where God is denied, finally nothing can be affirmed because no meaning exists.

The Renaissance and the Enlightenment began the enthronement of a dangerous undercurrent in Christendom, Hellenic thought, and philosophy. The New Testament usage of the Greek word *nomos* has reference to God's law, whereas in Greek thought it refers to the state's cultic regulations and ruling in general. We now have reduced, as of old, the meaning of law to the acts of state, whereas, from a Christian perspective, the State's enactments are only law when they conform to the word of God.

Because of the redefinition of all things now underway, *law* means simply the *present* stance of the State, nothing eternal nor absolutely true. Similarly, *faith* is losing its meaning. *Pistis, faith,* meant to the Greeks "a lower form of knowledge, believable testimony to be sure, but not a provable certainty." It had nothing to do with a man's relationship to God.[11] The Biblical meaning of *faith* is that it is a supernatural gift of God, whereby our refusal to acknowledge God and His truth is taken away and our eyes opened to the obvious truth of His being and works.

It is important to recognize that, as our world of meaning erodes, so too do words. The Third International Webster's Dictionary has not gained the usage its predecessors gained

---

9. Cited in John Lukaas, *Historical Consciousness*, (New York, N.Y.: Schocken Books, 1985), xv

10. *Ibid.*, 278ff.

11. Hans-Georg Gadamer, "Religion and Religiosity in Socrates," in John J. Cleary, editor, *Proceedings of the Boston Area Colloquium in Ancient Philosophy,* vol. I (Lanham, Maryland: University Press of America, 1986), 55.

simply because it erodes the concept of meaning. From a Christian as well as an empirical and historical perspective, *words* have meaning. They are prepositional truths. "Words tell a story."[12] From the perspective of the deconstructionists, words have a continually changing meaning, depending upon the reader, and they cannot be held to any fixed or proximate meaning. Given such views, we now face, as a society, the *planned* end of all communication.

Now the triune God of Scripture is the source of all definition and meaning. The origin of The Fall is Satan's temptation in Genesis 3:5, the claim that man can be is own god, knowing or defining for himself all good and evil, all law and morality, in short, *everything*. Self-definition now prevails among fallen men: they decide for themselves what is good or bad, and the result is that, instead of the common language of God's law and meaning, they have only their purely personal ideas and meanings. The result is the end of community, communion, and communication.

The artist Rene Magritte (d. 1967) is an example of this war against meaning. His paintings had no meaning: they simply *were*. "He considered his work successful when *no* explanation of causality or meaning can satisfy our curiosity."[13] His purpose was "to put the real world on trial."[14] As against any meaning available to all, there was no community of meaning. Nothing for him had a meaning in terms of a common world of meaning. Of his painting, he held "they *are* a meaning."[15] This means that *nothing* can be judged by anything nor by any standard beyond itself because it is its own meaning without any relationship to anything or anyone else. This is the logic of a world without God: all things are then simply *brute factuality*, to use Cornelius Van Til's term; they are totally meaningless and unrelated facts.

---

12. *Ibid.*, 39.
13. Suzi Gablik, *Magritte* (London, England: Thames and Hudson, 1970, 1985), 10.
14. *Ibid.*, 9.
15. *Ibid.*, 12.

This is the utter antithesis of communion, community, and communication. It is a denial of all ties to God and men. Whether it was the Surrealist school of artists, or Magritte, their works, and commonly their lives, were marked by "pure perversity."[16] This observation by Gablik tells us much about our time. Whether in art, education, politics, crime, or anything else in the modern spirit, including religion, *pure perversity* is its basic nature. The disintegration of the world around us is due to that spirit of pure perversity.

Magritte, as his own god, sought to separate himself from all of God's reality. In Gablik's words, "Magritte's paintings are a systematic attempt to disrupt any dogmatic view of the physical world."[17] Men in the anti-God tradition of Sade want a total separation from God's world into a realm of their own creation. They resent any world they never made. We have therefore not only a war being waged against Christianity, but against every element of God's creation. The goal is a plastic, a synthetic world totally made by man. Men seek to recreate mankind out of God's image into a self-image of every man's devising. This is what our grade school *values clarification* courses teach, and this is why homosexuality but not chastity is taught in our state schools.

The world knows that a war is being waged against Jesus Christ, but too many churchmen are unaware of the full dimensions of that war. It is total war, and so must our dedication to Christ our King be. Our Lord tells us, in Revelation 3:14-16,

> 14. And unto the angel of the church of the Laodiceans write; These things saith the Amen, the faithful and true witness, the beginning of the creation of God;
> I know thy works, that thou art neither cold nor hot: I would thou were cold or hot.
> So then because thou art lukewarm, and neither cold nor hot, I will spue thee out of my mouth.

---

16. *Ibid.*, 56.
17. *Ibid.*, 112.

Chapter 5

William Blake: "Everything that Lives is Holy"

One of the strange figures of English literature is William Blake (November 28, 1775 – August 12, 1827). Blake was both an appealing figure and a repulsive one, a devout Anglican in his love of the old order and also a Gnostic, for a time a Swedenborgian, and a parlor revolutionist. Like Swedenborg, who saw esoteric meanings in the Bible no one else could imagine, Blake saw esoteric meanings in everything. Blake was almost childish in his glee over every hidden and convoluted meaning advocated by heretics old and new. There seem also to be evidences of beliefs later formalized by the British-Israel or Identity movement. As for Blake, the Bible's prophesies were fulfilled in the British people and state.

There are intentional levels of meaning in Blake, but often there is an obvious and militant one. A work of great importance as revelatory of a development in the mind of the modern age is Blake's *The Marriage of Heaven and Hell* (1793). It was written at the time of the French Revolution, and its primary meaning reflects the fact.

Blake's mind was like a net that caught all the currents and drifting mental debris of his age. A key concept appears almost at once, and its statement is following a declaration that "a new heaven is begun."

> Without Contraries is no progression. Attraction and Repulsion, Reason and Energy, Love and Hate, are necessary to Human existence.
>
> From these contraries spring what the religious call Good & Evil. Good is the passive that obeys Reason, Evil is the Active springing from Energy.
>
> Good is Heaven. Evil is Hell.[1]

It is apparent from this that what Hegel formulated was very much in the intellectual atmosphere in Blake's day. Hegel's thesis-antithesis-synthesis system has its analogue in Blake's contraries. Moreover, to assume that Blake saw either contraries as bad, or heaven and hell as good and evil in the Christian sense would be very wrong. Long before Nietzsche, we have in Blake the transvaluation of all values. We will misunderstand Blake if we assume that he used language as we do. Blake read black where we read white.

Blake's "God" rarely appears in his writings; He is simply *being*. Secondary powers, as in gnosticism, are the forces that count. His is a pantheistic world in which demiurges rule. Blake's Christian "hang-over" makes him more ready to see sin as a reality, but his gnosticism leads him to see historical events rather than the Bible as revelation. The French Revolution was thus for him a great event in the spiritual world, more important than any Biblical event it would seem. The Christian virtues are replaced by Blake with pride and sensuality. Blake's hostility to popular Christianity was not in the name of a clear-cut Biblical faith but in terms of a contempt for those lacking in the secret knowledge. Blake used a variety of occult traditions without giving clear allegiance to any; he was his own prophet and religion. He gloried in his isolation and stressed it. He sought profundity in obscurity. In his drawings, his lines are clean and hard, whereas in his mystical

---

1. Geoffrey Keynes, editor, *Poetry and Prose of William Blake* (London, England: The Nonesuch Press, 1935), 191.

writings, clear, sharp knowledge gives way to blurred meanings.

At the near beginning of *The Marriage of Heaven and Hell*, Blake not only declares that "a new heaven is begun" but that "the eternal Hell revives." We have here his "contraries," so that Edom has now dominion, and we have "the return of Adam into Paradise."

Then Blake gives us a section on "The Voice of the Devil." He cites certain opinions as false, in particular the bipartite doctrine of men as body and soul. Many would agree with this without realizing that Blake's purpose is to unite man's being in "Energy," which is "Eternal Delight," meaning sexual desire. Restraint of desire is "Satanic" in appearance, but it is in reality otherwise. For Blake, both Christ and Satan champion desire, and in fact, the Comforter, or Holy Spirit, is Desire. Blake cites some of his "Proverbs of Hell," aphorisms designed to further a gnostic self-fulfillment in direct violation of moral considerations. Some of these proverbs are:

> Drive your car and your plow over the bones of the dead.
> The road of excess leads to the palace of wisdom.
> Prudence is a rich, ugly old maid courted by Incapacity.
> If the fool would persist in his folly he would become wise.
> Prisons are built with stones of Law; Brothels with bricks of Religion.
> The lust of the goat is the bounty of God. Exuberance is Beauty.
> Sooner murder an infant in its cradle than nurse unacted desires.[2]

These are clearly expressive of the Romantic mood. Virtue meant for the Romantics exuberance, and vice was unacted desire.

Blake then goes further: "All deities reside in the human breast." He then gives us "A Memorable Fancy," the prophets Isaiah and Ezekiel dining with Blake. Blake states that Isaiah told him, with respect to his visions,

---

2. *Ibid.*, 192-195.

> "I saw no God, nor heard any, in a finite organical perception; but my senses discover'd the infinite in everything, and as I was then persuaded, & remain confirm'd, that the voice of honest indignation is the voice of God, I cared not for consequences, but wrote."
>
> Then I asked: "does a firm persuasion that a thing is so, make it so?"
>
> He replied: "All poets believe that it does, & in ages of imagination this firm persuasion removed mountains; but many are not capable of a firm persuasion of any thing."[3]

The occult romantic imagination creates reality. We have here before Hegel his doctrine that the rational is the real. What man's mind intelligently and clearly conceives is thereby the real. Because of this, man's "honest indignation is the voice of God." We can understand from this why the Romantics saw themselves as true prophets. Their intense convictions and strong indignations were ipso facto *truth*.

This "Memorable Fancy" is preceded by a statement that gives the rationale for this view:

> The ancient Poets animated all sensible objects with Gods or Geniuses, calling them by the names and adorning them with the properties of woods, rivers, mountains, lakes, cities, nations, and whatever their enlarged & numerous senses could perceive.
>
> And particularly they studied the genius of each city & country, placing it under its mental deity;
>
> Till a system was formed, which some took advantage of, & enslave'd the vulgar by attempting to realize or abstract the mental deities from their objects: thus began Priesthood;
>
> Choosing forms of worship from poetic tales.
>
> And at length they pronounc'd that the Gods had order'd such things.
>
> Thus men forgot that All deities reside in the human breast.[4]

---

3. *Ibid.*, 195f.
4. *Ibid.*, 195.

This tells us how old the modern view of the birth of religions is! The beginning of occultism is that plenary power resides within the universe, not beyond it. This means that man must see this world and this life as complete, without reference to anything beyond it. The way back to the Garden of Eden, man's true innocence, is to transcend good and evil. Before Nietzsche, Blake insisted on the transvaluation of all values. Using the Biblical scheme in a radically different way, Blake wrote:

> The ancient tradition that the world will be consumed in fire at the end of six thousand years is true, as I have heard from Hell.
>
> For the cherub with the flaming sword is hereby commanded to leave his guard at tree of life; and when he does, the whole creation will be consumed and appear infinite and holy, whereas it now appears finite & corrupt.
>
> This will come to pass by an improvement of sensual enjoyment.[5]

The thesis of the "sexual revolution" of the 1960s was that mankind would be regenerated and energized by a total "freedom" for all kinds of sexuality. This "revolution" was an end product of Romanticism. The Romantic vision sees absolute freedom from restraint as the gateway to paradise. For Blake, his wife was a bar to his freedom to try polygamy.

Blake's thesis was this: "God only Acts & Is, in existing beings or Men."[6] He held, "I have also the Bible of Hell, which the world shall have whether they will or no."[7]

At the end of *The Marriage of Heaven and Hell*, Blake gives us "A Song of Liberty." Its theme is the coming destruction and annihilation of all law. The cleansing fires of man's inherent passions and desire will, when given freedom, make man a free creature in the new paradise. No more, Blake declared, let "pale religious lechery call that virginity that wishes but acts

---

5. *Ibid.*, 197.
6. *Ibid.*, 198.
7. *Ibid.*, 200.

not!"[8] By Blake's logic, one should be virtuous by murdering rather than suppressing the urge to kill! "The sons of joy" are the champions of unrestricted freedom.

Since the gods or God, and heaven and hell, are alike creations of man's mind, for man to oppose anything to his desires is evil. His mind must be reconciled to his body, to his desires and lusts, because only so can he be a whole man. Since all things have their origin in man, for man to oppose one aspect of his thinking or feeling to another is to torment himself. Since heaven and hell are alike his creation, projections of his imagination, he must unite them to be a whole man. Thus, he cannot oppose good to evil, morality to actions that are lawless, nor reason to passion.

Important also in this connection is Blake's *There is No Natural Religion* (c. 1788). Orthodox Christianity cannot accept natural religion because nature is fallen, and the fallen man's religion is closest to that of the Marquis de Sade. Paul, in Romans 1, tells us that fallen man holds, or holds down, the truth because of his unrighteousness or injustice. He prefers a religion in his own image. His "natural religion" is summed up in Genesis 3:5, his desire to be his own god and to *know* or establish his own doctrine of good and evil, law and morality. The Enlightenment concept of natural religion was of a Christianity without Christ and with a Deistic god; it was a step towards a full departure from a Biblical faith.

Blake's objection to natural religion was the antithesis of the Christian one. His "Argument" was "Man has no notion of moral fitness but from Education. Naturally he is only a natural organ subject to Sense."[9] St. Paul is by-passed. Man is a product of Nature whose only knowledge comes from his senses. Apart from education, he would have no knowledge of good and evil, nor a conscience. His religious and moral ideas are simply products of his education. Blake held, "Man's desires are limited by his perceptions, none can desire what he

8. *Ibid.*, 204.

9. William Blake, "There is no Natural Religion," First Series, in *Poetry and Prose of William Blake*, 147.

has not perceive'd."[10] All ideas, apart from education otherwise, are only empirically derived. This means that religion and morality, being aspects of education, are an imposition on the natural man, whether in Christian form or as man's natural religion.

The Infinite is God, and God "becomes as we are, that we may be as he is." We, when we see God as the Infinite in all things, see God and become a part of him.[11] "All religions are one," because "The Religions of all Nations are derived from each Nation's different reception of the Poetic Genius, which is every where call'd the Spirit of Prophecy." Because man is the source of all religions, they are essentially one. "The true Man is the source, he being the Poetic Genius."[12]

"After" Kant and Hegel, Blake saw the world as a product of his reason, or, his imagination. He thus conversed with angels, like Swedenborg, and, naturally, was not contradicted by any of his own creations. In fact, he was marvelously supported. Only Mrs. Blake, who, despite his efforts, was not his creature, ever contradicted him.

At the end of *The Marriage of Heaven and Hell*, there is a conclusion in seven words: "For every thing that lives is holy."[13] That sentence became, in the hands of Allen Ginsberg, a standard in the 1960s for the sexual revolution. It became a justification for every kind of sexual practice. Blake's sentence was not perverted. What Blake did not do, the sexual revolutionaries openly practiced.

If "everything that lives is holy," then, there is no need for law, because the concern of law is good and evil. The *unholy* and *anti-holy* is dealt with by law. If things as they are, the *status quo* in every realm, are holy, then the only problem is the person, such as the Christian, who insists that the world is fallen and evil, and, instead of affirming the *status quo*. God's law-order must be upheld and extended. The humanistic

---

10. *Idem.*
11. *Ibid.*, from "There is no Natural Religion. Second Series," 148.
12. *Ibid.*, "All Religions are One," c. 1788, 149.
13. Blake, *ibid.*, "The Marriage of Heaven and Hell," 204.

revolutionaries, given their logic, can only war against Christianity for affirming God's law, because the *status quo* of a fallen world is "good" for them. Logically, given their evolutionary faith, they should say that man need not have evolved out of the primeval slime, because it was in itself holy and beyond good and evil. Indeed, logically they should declare themselves content to return to the previous nothingness. No criterion can stand before their relativism.

The late Lenny Bruce was a champion of this anti-law, relativistic position. He declared,

> The religious leaders are "what *should be*.... Let me tell you the truth. The truth is 'what is.' If 'what is' is, you have to sleep eight, ten hours a day, that is the truth. A lie will be: People need no sleep at all. Truth is 'what is.' [14]

William Blake was a militant antinomian. His hostility at times to the churches and to Christians was due to the fact that the churches then still affirmed theonomy, the rule of God's law. Blake, in "The Everlasting Gospel" (c. 1818), gives us his version of the woman taken in adultery being brought to Jesus for judgment.

> Jesus was sitting in Moses' Chair,
> They brought the trembling Woman There.
> Moses commands she be stoned to death,
> What was the sound of Jesus' breath?
> He laid His hand on Moses' Law:
> The Ancient Heavens, in Silent Awe
> Writ with curses form Pole to Pole,
> All away began to roll:
> The Earth trembling & Naked lay
> In secret bed of Mortal Clay,
> On Sinai felt the hand divine
> Putting back the bloody shrine,
> And she heard the breath of God
> As she heard by Eden' flood:
> "Good & Evil are no more!
> Sinai's trumpets, cease to roar!

---

[14] Lenny Bruce, "How to Talk Dirty and Influence People," *Playboy*, vol. II, no. 1. January, 1964, 182.

Come, finger of God, to write!
The Heavens are not clean in thy Sight.
Thou art God, & thou Alone;
Nor may the sinner cast one stone.
To be Good only, is to be
A God or else a Pharisee.
Thou Angel of the Presence Divine
Thou didst create this Body of Mine,
Wherefore has thou writ these Laws
And Created Hell's dark jaws?
My Presence I will take from thee:
A Cold Leper thou shalt be …"[15]

Not only does Blake use the name of Jesus to affirm that all things are holy, he insists that "to be Good only, is To be a God or else a Pharisee." This does not say much for his view of God, who is equated with a Pharisee! Even more, Blake, has rendered relative the ideas of good and evil, tells us Men need to be *both* good and evil. The truly holy life means one that freely and happily affirms and practices all things. It means living beyond the old definitions of good and evil by affirming both to be a part of life. Heaven and hell are married; men can feel free to practice those things which were once regarded as evil, depraved, and hellish because no real line of division separates good and evil.

For Blake, this meant no more perhaps than wanting a loving relationship with another woman while loving his wife. His philosophy, however, had no such limitation. Others pursued the doctrine to radical conclusions.

In the late 1930s and into the 1940s, I knew a seminary professor who had fought vigorously for a "liberal" view of the Bible. He wanted a limited skepticism concerning the Bible, but not about the supernatural Jesus. When his successors reduced Jesus to a natural man, and eliminated all traces of supernaturalism as mythical, he was shocked and outraged. He failed to recognize that men cannot set eternal and binding landmarks and boundaries. Only God can. Having substituted

15. Blake, *op. cit.*, "The Everlasting Gospel," 139;

his boundary for God's, he was appalled that men were transgressing it.

So too with churchmen after Blake. By denying the permanent validity of God's law, they broke the human limitation God had ordained. Antinomianism took command of the churches, and there was no bulwark against the flood of moral relativism that followed. If modernism is justified, why not Blake also, and Lenny Bruce, Hugh Hefner, and others? How can our affirmations of what is good and what is evil survive if we deny God's law? If God has no boundaries, how can man have them? If good and evil are both relative concepts, not eternal verities, then *Man is the absolute.* This is then, and has been, the logical conclusion, every man his own law, and his own world.

Chapter 6

The Spirit of the Age

In Genesis 3:4-5, we are told what the tempter's program was; "Ye shall not surely die. For God doth know that in the day ye eat thereof, then your eyes shall be opened, and ye shall be as gods, knowing good and evil." Understanding the meaning of this is of central importance, because accepting this premise is man's original sin and is basic to all fallen men. Failure to understand these words warps the whole of the Bible. Lester J. Kuyper called attention some years ago, to the meaning of "to know good and evil." "It simplifies the right or authority to exercise independent discrimination between right and wrong."

> The tempter (Gen. 3:5) explains that partaking of the fruit of the tree of knowledge of good and evil would make the woman like God, a knower of good and evil. In the light of our interpretation this means that man was induced to take divine prerogatives in his own hand and set up his own moral order. The attractiveness of this independence from all restraints caught the fancy of the human pair and they arrogated to themselves that authority which only Yahweh has and exercises.

> The observation (3:22) that man has become like God to know good and evil is therefore not irony but sober reality. Man had taken to himself a right which is God's. God had delegated to man his realm of dominion, the created world. Man broke the confines of his realm to enter the dominion of God. That became the first manifestation of sin.
>
> Man's refusal to subject himself to God has been the basic nature of sin from Adam to our time.[1]

Instead of being subject to God's moral order, man chose and chooses to create his own moral order, to make laws on his own and to declare what is good and bad, right or wrong for himself, in terms of his own desires. Man can therefore justify himself in any sin or crime in terms of his personal interests, and he sees his will as primary and determinative. The term, *reasons of state,* is a familiar one; *raisons d'etat* means that the interests of the state take priority over God's law. We can speak also of *the interests of man* as commonly being given clear and plain predominance over the laws of God. Our original sin leads us always to see our will as determinative. Only the grace of God through Jesus Christ can break our will and supplant the old Adam in us with the new man, a new creation (2 Cor. 5:17).

The whole of man's history is his attempt to create a new paradise on earth by his own fiat will. The *garden* theme is a common one in ancient history, as is the urge to utopia in the modern era. Man wants a paradise without God and on his own terms; he wants a new world order without God. His Towers of Babel are many, and very much with us.

The whole history of redemption is the struggle between God's determination of good and evil, and man's will to create his own world order based on his definition of good and evil. The Bible describes it as the war between God's true Jerusalem and man's Babylon; Augustine saw it as the war between the city of man and the city of God.

---

1. Lester J. Kuyper, "To Know Good and Evil," in *Interpretation, A Journal of Bible and Theology*, October, 1947, vol. I, no. 4, 492.

In this struggle, the city of man, fallen humanity, moves militantly towards its goal. An early Unitarian in the United States, Octavius Brooks Frothingham (1822-1895), held that true life meant unity with humanity rather than some supernatural God or Savior. Separation from humanity he saw as a living death:

> Humanity has but one life, breathes but one atmosphere, draws sustenance form one central orb. To be reconciled with humanity, to feel the common pulse, is life; to be alienated from humanity, to have no share in the common vitality is death. The slightest material separation is felt disastrously.[2]

Frothingham transferred the life-giving attributes of God to humanity. Similarly, he transferred the doctrine of the Holy Spirit to "the interior spirit of any age" and infallibility from God and His word to the spirit of an age:

> The interior spirit of any age is the spirit of God; and no faith can be living that has that spirit against it; no Church can be strong except in that alliance. The life of the time appoints the creed of the time and modifies the establishment of the time.[3]

For Frothingham, God is "the human in all men."[4] This is, of course, the essence of religious modernism: it takes its gospel from the spirit of the age. Whatever the spirit of the age decrees, the mindless modernists pompously echo. They are thus for abortion, homosexuality, euthanasia, and whatever else the spirit of the age decrees.

In terms of the Frothingham-gospel, and the Sadean order, nothing can legitimately stand in the way of the spirit of the age. Sade opposed his anarchistic will against all orders of all ages, but he would have agreed with Frothingham in opposing any supernatural law being imposed on man. For both

---

2. Octavius Brooks Frothingham, *The Religion of Humanity* (New York, N.Y.: G.P. Putnam's sons, 1875. Third Edition), 130.

3. *Ibid.*, 7f.

4. O.B. Frothingham, *The Safest Creed and Twelve Other Recent Discourses of Reason* (New York, N.Y.: Butts, 1874), 179f.

Frothingham and Sade, the ultimate law was this: *man's will be done.*

"The interior spirit of any age," i.e., the man-derived imperative, is that of Genesis 3:5, man's will be to be his own god and law, determining all things according to his desires. This, however, is death to progress. If the spirit of the age demands that murder, slavery, the communization of property, money, and women be decreed, it cannot be legitimately opposed, given the premise of Frothingham. Sade would at all times and in all things oppose any restraint. Frothingham's premise is a door leading to Sade's world.

The Biblical premise that all men are sinners, fallen and totally depraved (i.e., every aspect of their being tainted and governed by sin) has in its favor the authority of God and history. The premise of Frothingham is Darwinian: man is evolving onward and upward, so that progress is inevitable. What Christians call *sin* is a relic of his evolutionary past. For Freud, it was man's id and ego that governed him, both relics of the primeval horde. But Freud saw no escape from man's past. The will to death, man's self-judgment, would always prevail over his pleasure principle, the will to live.

On varying grounds, Freud's pessimism has won the humanistic day. In some quarters hope for man's future arouses cynical scorn. Whereas in the early days of Darwin the Christian view of man was seen as false and pessimistic, now the Christian view of man as redeemable, and history leading to the great victory of the Kingdom of God over the kingdom of man is now seen as wildly optimistic. The spirit of the age gives man a weathervane orientation.

We see one facet of this in American law and the U.S. Supreme Court and its decision. These are increasingly politically and/or populistically governed, and the Court shows little embarrassment at its unstable stance. For lack of an objective and absolute standard, the courts (and civil governments) face a growing cynicism and contempt. We can see the difference by considering the dying words of Somerset before being beheaded. Thomas Seymour, or Lord Seymour of Sudeley (c. 1508-49), was indeed a proud and ambitious man. Today, he would probably retire with a large pension and much public honor. Then, he faced Tudor "justice," but he died, declaring,

> Masters and good fellows, I am come hither for to die, but a true and faithful man as any was unto the King's Majesty, and to his realm. But I am condemned by a law whereunder I am subject, and as we all; and therefore to show obedience I am content to die; wherewith I am well content, being a thing mostly heartily welcome unto me; for the which I do thank God.... For as I am a man, I have deserved at God's hand many deaths, and it hath pleased his goodness, whereas he might have taken me (so) suddenly that I should neither have known him nor myself, thus now to visit me and call me with this present death as you see, when I have had time to remember and knowledge (know) him, and to know also myself; for which thing I do thank him most heartily.[5]

So saying, he knelt, saying thrice, "Jesus, save me." The executioner severed his head with a single blow.

He died with a serenity because he knew there was an absolute justice and an assured Redeemer, Jesus Christ. Men today can face little with peace because they are not at peace with God. Their "peace" is with the spirit of the age, and it leaves them with nothing. Men determine for themselves what is good and evil, but their decisions give them no peace because this is still God's world. God is still their Judge, and not they their own.

The tempter's "plan" for man's freedom in Genesis 3:5 destroyed the Garden of Eden. The same plan is no less destructive today. An order created by Christians is crumbling under the anarchy of self-will and deliberate immoralism. We are told in Judges 21:25 that in that era, "there was no king in Israel: every man did that which was right in his own eyes." Having rejected God as their King in favor of their own will

---

5. Joseph Allen Matter, *Rule by King or Rule by Law* (New York, N.Y.: Vantage Press, 1979), 185.

and self-rule, they ended in slavery. We in our time see every man doing what is right in his own eyes, and the consequences are rapidly appearing.

Chapter 7

Whatever Is, Is

Alexander Pope (1688-1744) introduced Deistic ideas that are with us still. A loyal Catholic, Pope better represented the world of neo-classicism and Deism than he did his church. He is perhaps best know for the concluding paragraph of his "An Essay on Man:"

> X. Cease then, nor ORDER imperfection name:
> Our proper bliss depends on what we blame.
> Know thy own point: This kind, this due degree
> Of blindness, weakness, Heaven bestows on thee.
> Submit. — In this, or any other sphere,
> Secure to be as blest as thou canst bear:
> Safe in the hand of one disposing Power,
> Or in the natal, or the mortal hour,
> All nature is but art, unknown to thee;
> All chance, direction, which thou canst not see;
> All discord, harmony not understood;
> A partial evil, universal good:
> And, spite of pride, in erring reason's spite,
> One truth is clear, WHATEVER IS, IS RIGHT.

Pope believes in a cosmic providence, but it is not a Christian providence; rather, it is a trust in the total goodness of the natural order as created by the Deistic divinity. In fact, evil for

Pope is good when rightly understood. If we but only understood, our greatest evil is our greatest good. Self-love thus pays dividends. ("Essay on Man," Second Epistle, II.) We can understand from this why the idea arose that, if each pursues his own economic self-interest, the good of all will result. There is a connection between such thinking and Adam Smith.

Pope's idea is a perversion of Romans 8:28: "And we know that all things work together for good to them that love God, to them who are the called according to his purpose." The Bible, however, makes clear that this marvelous providence applies *only* to the ones who love God and are His called and elect ones. For the reprobate, we are told, "As thou hast done, it shall be done unto thee: thy reward shall return upon thine own head" (Obadiah 15; see also Lamentations 1:22; Jeremiah 50:29). Paul speaks of the belief that if we do evil, good will come, as a doctrine of damnation (Rom. 3:8).

It was precisely this perverse doctrine that Deism, and, later Transcendentalism asserted. Ralph Waldo Emerson held, "that even in a brothel man is on his way to all that 'is great & good.'"[1] Given this doctrine, why should man ever repent of his sins, or mind his ways? Everything he does leads "to all that is great and good," and his evil keeps him on track to it.

This perverse doctrine led often to a remarkable moral blindness. After all, why be upset over great evils when thy lead inevitably to the greater good for all? For an example of this, consider Anthony Trollope. At the time of the great famine in Ireland in the mid-1800s he ridiculed reports of its horrors. On top of that, he was fond of quoting Pope's sentence, "Whatever is, is right." His brother, Thomas Trollope, made it his personal motto.[2] Would an enslaved man, or a man in a Marxist slave labor camp, agree with Pope's sentiment? It is the dogma of comfortable, philosophizing men.

---

1. Joseph Slater, editor, *The Correspondence of Emerson and Carlyle* (New York, N.Y.: Columbia University Press, 1964, 1965), 39.
2. Victoria Glendinning, *Anthony Trollope* (New York, N.Y.: Alfred A. Knopf, 1993), 185n.

The world being sinful and fallen, this failure to recognize evil in all men, including us, is a most dangerous yet common affliction, and a self-chosen one. Whether affirmed by Alexander Pope, Anthony Trollope, Lenny Bruce, or anyone else, it is a doctrine of smugness and moral obtuseness.

The ideas expressed by Pope were not original with him. A generation earlier, they had been stated philosophically by Gottfried Wilhelm Leibniz (1646-1716). Leibniz was deeply immersed in Rosicrucianism and Jewish Kabbalism, all of which made him alien to the transcendent God of Scripture. Voltaire, in *Candide*, satirized Leibniz doctrine of "all is for the best in this best of all possible worlds." Bertrand Russell's analysis (1900) of Leibniz did not rescue him from this strand in his philosophy. It was Leibniz's mathematics that Russell respected. It will help us to place Leibniz, if we realize that for him Jesus Christ was the Cabalists' Adam Kamon.[3]

John S. Feinberg rightly saw Leibniz as thoroughly at odds with theonomy. Leibniz held reason to be ultimate, and therefore God's possibilities were for him reason's possibilities. "Leibniz is quick to claim that something absolutely contrary is imaginable but cannot exist."[4] Feinberg pointed out,

> It is of crucial importance to note Leibniz' emphasis on the idea that God did not create the concepts of the possibles or possible essences. They are co-eternal with His own existence. As Leibniz conceives the matter, creation is the actualization of possibilities…
>
> …In Leibniz' rationalistic theology, a God prior to the possibles would present a problem. Leibniz handles such a problem by means of his metaphysical conceptions as to the co-eternality of the forms with God.[5]

---

3. G.W. Leibniz, "Freedom of Man in the Origin of Evil," in *Theodicy* (London, England: Routtedge & Kegan. 1951), 133.
4. John S. Feinberg, *Theologies and Evil* (Washington, D.C.: University Press of America, 1979), 29.
5. *Ibid.*, 30, 31.

Supposedly, in this neoplatonic scheme, the forms are equal in ultimacy with God. In reality the forms are superior because they limit God but cannot be limited by Him. "Leibniz claims that God operates according to the principle of sufficient reason." God's actions, then, are always rationally determined and never arbitrary."[6] Well before Kant and Hegel, Leibniz believed that the rational is the real. For Leibniz, a concept of God as absolute and the determiner of all things in terms of His sovereign and unconditional will was anathema. He wrote, "Our end is to banish from men the false ideas that represent God to them as an absolute prince employing a despotic power."[7] Such a God he held is "unfitted to be loved and unworthy of being loved."[8] Leibniz' God was a philosophical concept, not the living God of the Biblical revelation. Leibniz did not want a God who could disturb the tranquility of his rational thinking. As a result, he sought an explanation of evil in rationality, not in sin, in logical formulations, not in the fall of man. Leibniz's philosophy needed God as a limiting concept, not as absolute Lord over all. In time, "science" would provide mechanisms whereby those who came after Leibniz could dispense with God. This disengagement with God appears in Leibniz's thinking:

> I have shown already (part I, no. 86 seq.) that souls cannot spring up naturally, or be derived from one another, and that it is necessary that ours either be created or be pre-existent. I have even pointed out a certain middle way between a creation and an entire pre-existence… Nevertheless it will be well to add that I would dispense with miracles in the generating of man, as in that of the other animals.[9]

The God of Scripture and Biblical theology is of no use to Leibniz except as an occasional crutch to validate his thinking with no commitment on his part. Austin Farrer rightly stated that "his dogmatic ancestry is to be looked for in Thomism and

6. *Ibid*,. 34, 35.
7. Leibniz, *op. cit.*, 127.
8. *Idem.*
9. *Ibid.*, 361.

Catholic humanism as much as anywhere."[10] Moreover, "It is a natural mistake for the student of seventeenth century thought to underestimate the tenacity of scholastic Aristotelianism."[11] Leibniz had scholastic teaching.

Leibniz's philosophy told him that we live in the best of all possible worlds, *not* in a radically fallen and depraved world at war with God. In Leibniz there is evident a process of disengagement from the sovereign God of Scripture *and* from Scripture. How can a fallen world be the best of all possible worlds? How can fallen man, in separation from God, determine what true and Right Reason is? By thinking non-theologically, Leibniz began a departure from reality. If the Fall is the basic fact about fallen man's orientation, how can this man's perspective be other than warped? Man, having separated himself from God, has forsaken true reason and communication.

Early in the Twentieth Century, the Dada Manifesto declared, "Art is a private matter; the artist does it for himself, any work of art that can be understood is the product of a journalist." And *Transition* said, "the artist expresses, he does not communicate."[12] This is the aesthetic counterpart to Sade's philosophy. Communication, ethics, aesthetics, art, and more, all are dead because the world is reduced to private sensations.

If *whatever is, is right*, then there is a total equality of all things, of all factuality. Then, equally, *whatever is, is wrong*, because total equality marks everything. But, above all, what all this means is that all things being equal, all things are meaningless. If morality is a private option, then theft, rape, and murder cannot be judged, as Sade concluded. If *whatever is, is right*, then nothing is right because all things are then meaningless. Meaning begins with differentiation, when we

---

10. *Ibid.*, "Editor's Introduction," 11.

11. *Ibid.*, 12.

12. Allen A. Block, *Anonymous Toil, A Re-evaluation of the American Radical Novel in the Twentieth Century*, (Lanham, Maryland: University Press of America, 1992), 50.

say *one* is not *fourteen*, and *nothing* is not *everything*. The equality of all things is the meaninglessness of all things.

But the modern world is hostile to meaning, so much so that some of its sons call themselves *post-modernists*, meaning that they are beyond good and evil, beyond meaning.

We are, then, in the world of whatever is, is, if we can even say that it *is*.

Chapter 8

Percy Bysshe Shelley

Percy Bysshe Shelley (1792-1822) had much in common with the Marquis de Sade while representing a variation of humanism. Humanism after Rousseau was vocal in its belief in the natural goodness of man. As against Calvin's insistence on fallen man's total depravity, Rousseau believed in the natural man's goodness when not corrupted by family and church, these two being the essence of a chaining civilization. The Enlightenment had been the return of Renaissance humanism; it was the humanism of men who were "enlightened" and so regarded the emphasis on family and church as best suited for the ignorant masses. Many of the key Enlightenment men never married.

Shelley never doubted his goodness. He was regularly disappointed that those around him who displeased him lacked his virtues.

Basic to the neo-classical writers, and more pronounced in the Romantics, is the theme of *solitude*. In a world corrupted by family and church, the two institutions of an oppressive Christianity, the "free" man was lonely. This Romantic hero, faced with an ugly and hostile civilization, resigned, we are told,

> … his high and holy soul
> to images of the majestic past,
> That paused within his passive being now,
> Like winds that bear sweet music, when they breathe
> Through some dim latticed chamber.[1]

These lines come from "Alastor, or Spirit of Solitude." For the Romantics, the "high and holy soul" is always lonely, and solitude is his lot. He cannot live in peace with or in community with the vast world of baser men. As a result, his is a professionally lonely man. The culmination of this is indeed hell. Jean-Paul Sartre, in *No Exit*, has Garcin declare, "Hell is—other people!" Albert William Levi commented,

> Hell is other people for Sartre because in his quaint universe of appropriation and domination (a land of Hobbesian state of nature where the stakes are not the externals of wealth and deference but purely internal states of consciousness like nausea, shame, pride, and alienation) all contact with the Other implies a latent contest.[2]

"Alastor" is a pretentious poem, Shelley sees himself not only as a "high and holy soul," but as too good for humanity, or even life. He can commune only with nature. His opening line salutes "Earth, ocean, air, beloved brotherhood!" Where humanity is concerned, he can communicate only with the noble dead:

> I have made my bed
> In charnels and on coffins, where black death
> Keeps record of the trophies won from thee,
> Hoping to still these obstinate questionings
> Of thee and thine, by forcing some lone ghost
> Thy messenger, to render up the tale
> Of what we are.[3]

---

1. *John Keats and Percy Bysshe Shelley, Complete Poetical Works* (New York, N.Y.: The Modern Library, n.d.), 16.
2. Albert William Levi, *Philosophy and the Modern World* (Bloomington, Indiana University Press, 1959), 420.
3. Shelly, *op. cit.*, 2f.

Shelly came from a notable family, and he enraged his father. Had he come of common stock, perhaps some healthy laughter might have recalled him to reality. As it happened, he dreamed of "reforming the world."

The Marquis de Sade saw Rousseau's Nature without any Christian borrowings. It was without morality and was for him the area for natural man's unhindered self-expression. All that occurs in Nature was held to be normative, and whatever went against that normal expression, i.e., Christianity was unnatural and therefore to be forbidden. For Shelley and the Romantics, Nature was on the side of the rebel against family and church. For Shelley, "nature's inner shrine" was "where gods and fiends in worship bend."[4] The God of Christianity is replaced by pagan "gods and fiends," by natural, anti-Christian forces.

Everything in Shelley drew him to the myth of Prometheus, the Titan who defied Jupiter or Zeus, the supreme god. Prometheus was a favorite of the Romantics; like him, they were in revolt against heaven. Like him, they felt chained, in their cases to the conventional society of family and church. Prometheus is the champion of liberty against the gods, himself a godlike being. Greek humanism in Aeschylus made Prometheus a hero without formally breaking with Zeus worship. The Romantics saw their Prometheus in revolt against the Biblical God. Philo M. Buck, Jr. said of the Romantic Prometheus,

> As a hero Prometheus was the more congenial to an age that understood Rouseau's *Social Contract* and Godwin's *Political Justice*, because he could so easily be made to symbolize human benevolence, and his great and triumphant opponent, Jupiter, lawless tyranny. Prometheus, the new and benevolent creed of liberty, equality, and fraternity, and sweetness and light; Jupiter the *ancien regime* of irresponsible power and blind ignorance.[5]

---

4. *Ibid.*, "The Daemon of the World," II. 96f., 21.
5. Philo M. Buck, Jr., *The World's Great Age* (New York, N.Y.: Macmillan, 1936), 83.

Prometheus Unbound is about the redemption of man, but, unlike Dante's *Divine Comedy*, it is a redemption *from* God. Man's harmony and perfection come by means of deliverance from God. Man's bondage to God is evil; his deliverance is into perfection. Shelley gives us a cleaned up version of the same revolution as de Sade's; it is presented as an invitation to all "noble souls." The Marquis summoned people to total sexual anarchism; Shelley's vision of the liberation of man is into a stateless, Godless world of licentious bliss and a peaceable realm of fulfillment for all. The "Earth" tells Prometheus, "Thou art more than God, being wise and kind."[6] Shelley sees himself as a Prometheus who unshackles himself and offers mankind freedom also.

In Shelley's work, Demogoron deposes Jupiter and sends him crying into hell. Ocean then hails the blissful world which follows the fall of Jupiter, the great god:

> Henceforth the fields of heaven-reflecting sea
> Which are my realm, will heave, unstained with blood,
> Beneath the uplifting winds, like plains of corn
> Swayed by the summer air; my streams will flow
> Round many-peopled continents, and round
> Fortunate isles; and from their glassy thrones
> Blue Proteus and his humid nymphs shall mark
> The shadow of fair ships, as mortals see
> The floating bark of the light-laden moon,
> With that white star, its sightless pilot's crest,
> Borne down the rapid sunset's ebbing sea;
> Tracking their path no more by blood and groans,
> And desolation, and the mingled voice
> Of slavery and command; but by the light
> of wave- reflected flowers, and floating odours,
> And music soft, and mild, free, gentle voices,
> And sweetest music, such as spirits love.[7]

This deliverance from the rule of heaven was the Romantic dream, and also the goal of revolutions. In the mid-1930s a professor of literature cited Shelley's "Prometheus Unbound"

---

6. Shelley, *op. cit.,* 232; "Prometheus Unbound," Act I, II. 144f.
7. *Ibid.*, 268; Act III, Scene II, ll. 18-34.

as a part of the "prophetic" literature in the background of the Russian Revolution. Such a radical revolution was an aspect of the Romantic hope, although, men such as Shelley would have become early victims.

Shelley's ideas were obviously anti-Christian. He gave to Christianity only a negative part in the shaping of Western civilization. He wrote, in the "Preface" to "Hellas,"

> We are all Greeks. Our laws, our literature, our religion, our arts have their root in Greece. But for Greece — Rome, the instructor, the conqueror, or the metropolis of our ancestors, would have spread no illumination with her arms, and we might still have been savages and idolaters; or, what is worse, might have arrived at such a stagnant and miserable state of social institution as China and Japan possess.[8]

For men like Shelley, Christianity and Christendom were only a "Middle" era between ancient and modern humanism. The evils produced by this humanism in the French and Russian Revolutions are not discussed; somehow, Christianity is to blame for them. Adolf Hitler's obvious ideal was classical civilization and its art.[9] Somehow, Christianity was seen as responsible for Hitler!

For Shelley, ancient Greece represented "perfection."[10] One of the "actors" in "Hellas" is Christ, who speaks of "Plato's sacred light, Of which my spirit was a burning marrow."[11] Christ, together with Satan and Mohamet, is a member of "The senate of the Gods."! The "God" of "Hellas" is a Greek conception. A Greek "semichorus I" tells us:

> In the great morning of the world,
> The Spirit of God with might unfurled
> The flag of Freedom over Chaos,
>   And all its banded anarchs fled,
> Like vultures frighted from Imaus,

8. *Ibid.*, 501; Preface to "Hellas."
9. Peter Adam, *Art of the Third Reich* (New York, N.Y.: Harry N. Abrams, 1992).
10. *Idem.*
11. *Ibid.*, Prologue, l. 94f.

Before an earthquake's tread.—
So from Time's tempestuous dawn
Freedom's spendour burst and shone:—
Thermopylae and Marathon
Caught, like mountains beacon-lighted,
The springing Fire.—The winged glory
On Philippi half-alighted,
Like an eagle on a promontory.
Its unwearied wings could fan
The quenchless ashes of Milan.
From age to age, form man to man,
It lived; and lit from land to land
Florence, Albion, Switzerland.[12]

The freedom was quenched. However, in Shelley's day Greece was struggling for freedom from Turkey. Shelley hoped that a new classical age would begin. With Greece arising once again, the Chorus could declare

The world's great age begins anew,
The golden years return,
The earth doth like a snake renew
Her winter weeds outworn:
Heaven smiles, and faiths and empires gleam,
Like wrecks of a dissolving dream.[13]

Shelley, a Romantic to the core of his being, saw liberation as deliverance from God, from family and church. Somehow, a world without Christianity would be the reign of freedom and bliss. In the world of the Marquis de Sade, all men are like himself eager to violate every law of God and man. Shelley wanted to reserve to himself that freedom from God's law, and yet he wanted to expel God from this world. Like the other Romantics, he lacked Sade's sense of consequences.

---

12. *Ibid.* 509; ll, 46-63.
13. *Ibid.*, 533, ll, 1060-1065.

Chapter 9

Lord Byron

John Milton's *Paradise Lost* (1674) gives us an important view of Satan as one who chooses evil as his good:

> ... but of this be sure,
> To do aught good never will be our task,
> But ever to do ill our sole delight,
> As being the contrary to his high will
> Whom we resist. If then his Providence
> Out of our evil seek to bring forth good,
> Our labour must be to pervert that end,
> And of good still to find means of evil.[1]

As against God's Providence, which makes all things work together for good to the chosen of God (Rom. 8:28), Satan decrees that the enemies of God must seek to create an evil providence, one that perverts God's purposes and makes them evil. As Camus has said, because God chooses good, we must choose evil.

Milton's Satan stresses that his choice is what God calls evil. He asserts the transvaluation of all values and all morality:

> ... Hail horrors, hail

1. John Milton, *Paradise Lost,* Book I, ll. 158-165.

> Infernal world, and thou profoundest Hell
> Receive thy new Possessor: One who brings
> A mind not to be chang'd by Place or Time.
> The mind is its own place, and in itself
> Can make a Heav'n of Hell, a Hell of Heav'n.
> What matter where, if I be still the same,
> And what I should be, all but less than he
> Whom Thunder hath made greater? Here at least
> We shall be free; th' Almighty hath not built
> Here for his envy, will not drive us hence:
> Here we may reign secure, and in my choice
> To reign is worth ambition through in Hell:
> Better to reign in Hell, than serve in Heav'n.[2]

These lines make clear that Milton was an unwitting father of the Romantic movement. The Romantics took their cue from Milton's Satan in their thinking and posturing. They made evil their good; rebellion became a virtue, and the solitude of evil, its separation from God and man, became a mark of virtue and of heroism. The mind became for Romanticism, poetically and philosophically, (as in Descartes, Berkeley, Hume, Kant, Hegel, and others), their real world. Theirs was "a mind not to be changed by Place or Time." The creative mind of man would make its own world.

Certainly this was true of George Gordon Byron (1788-1824). Not only did Lord Byron enjoy evil, he seemed to revel in giving the impression of a defiant contempt for morality and restrictions on his anarchic freedom. Like all the Romantics, he had a sharp eye for evil, not to condemn it really, but to call attention to the fact that the leaders of society were evil men. Thus, in the poem, "The Devil's Drive," he portrays the Devil as leaving the earth in shock because he sees greater evil in Parliament than in Hell. Byron is delighted to report on this "fact." Since Byron's many sins may have included incest, and he made sure we would think so, his concern with sin was not a moral one. In his poem "To Belshazzar," he condemns that ruler as "Unfit to govern, live, or die." Byron wanted in all

---

2. *Ibid.*, I, ll. 250-263.

things a heroic confrontation with judgment, a defiance of God and man.

Byron cultivated an offensive manner, as in his "Epitaph" which asked men to urinate on the grave of Robert Stewart, Marquis of Londonderry (Viscount Castlereagh) 1739-1821, one of England's more important leaders. Old and mentally disordered, he committed suicide. He had been, among other things, Napoleon's nemesis. But what did Byron say in his "Epitaph"?

Posterity will ne'er survey
  A nobler grave than this:
Here lie the bones of Castlereagh:
    Stop, traveler___________.

Byron took a childish pride in such things. Very early, the Romantic movement manifested a delight in vulgarity and crudity which in time became pornographic. The Romantics posed as martyrs while revelling, in most cases, in cruel insults and bad conduct. They were thin-skinned to criticism and voluble in insults.

Byron wrote some "Poems on Napoleon." He was drawn to losers. The victorious to him, as to Milton's Satan, were the repressive forces of the world. King Saul, Napoleon, Sardanapalus, Manfred, Cain, and like persons were at the center of his poetic vision. This was a form of rebellion against both God and man to look at the losers of history rather favorably. Those whom the Bible would see as the enemies of God, the Romantic mind was determined to declare heroic.

The Romantic mind loved suffering more than joy, and it regarded the destiny of the sensitive soul to be one of suffering. Byron concluded his poem "Euthanasia" with these words:

Count o'er the joys thine hours have seen,
  Count o'er thy days from anguish free,
And know, whatever thou has been,
  Tis something better not to be.

With solitude and suffering, the Romantic also indulged in "passion," and Byron rightly described Rousseau as the source of this:

> Here the self-torturing sophist, wild Rousseau
> The apostle of affliction, he who threw
> Enchantment over passion, and from woe
> Wrong overwhelming eloquence, first drew
> The breath which made him wretched; yet he knew
> How to make madness beautiful, and cast
> O'er erring deeds and thoughts, a heavenly hue
> Of words, like sunbeams, dazzling as they past
> The eyes, which o'er them shed tears feelingly and fast.[3]

The determined melancholy and isolation of the Romantic is described repeatedly. Life in "this world of woe" (Canto III,V) is a grim ordeal for the aristocratic Romantic; his only community is with Nature:

> The desert, forest, cavern, breaker's foam,
> Were unto him companionship, they spake
> A mutual language, clearer than the tome
> Of his land's tongue, which he would oft forsake
> For Nature's pages glass'd by sunbeams on the lake.[4]

The Romantic person was too good for fellowship with men; he communed instead with his god, Nature. To be isolated from mankind Byron saw as nobility:

> I live not in myself, but I become
> Portion of that around me; and to me,
> High mountains are a feeling, but the hum
> Of human cities torture; I can see
> Nothing to loathe in nature, save to be
> A link reluctant in a fleshly chain,
> Class'd among creatures, when the soul can flee.
> And with the sky, the peak, the heaving plain
> Of ocean, or the stars, mingle, and not in vain.[5]

The Romantic contempt for humanity meant in the French Revolution a desire to kill many as unwanted. In Max Stirner

---

3. "Childe Harold's Pilgrimage," Canto the Third, LXXVII.
4. *Ibid.*, III, XIII.
5. *Ibid.*, III, LXXII.

and Friedrich Nietzsche, it was a contempt for mankind, and Karl Marx saw the future as one that revolutionary leaders would mold, together with mankind.

In words that echo Macbeth regarding Banquo's issue, Byron's Childe Harold, says,

> I have not loved the world, nor the world me;
> I have not flatter'd its rank breath, nor bow'd
> To its idolatries a patient knee,—
> Nor coin'd my cheek to smiles,—nor cried aloud
> Its worship of an echo; in the crowd
> They could not deem me one of such; I stood
> Among them, but not of them; in a shroud
> Of thoughts which were not their thoughts, and still could,
> Had I not filed my mind, which thus it self subdued.[6]

For Byron, all humanity has bad breath, but apparently his breath is scented with violets!

In "Lara," Canto I, XVII f., we have a vivid portrait of the Romantic hero: isolated, hated, enigmatic, filled with "a vital scorn of all," fiery passion, and more. To despise the common herd was a necessary qualification for heroic man. Byron's Manfred, in fact, denies connection with humanity, declaring,

> Patience and patience! Hence—that word was made
> For brutes of burthen, not for birds of prey;
> Preach it to mortals of a dust like thine—
> I am not of thine order.[7]

When men renounce God and His law, they renounce their humanity. Men who make laws for themselves or for others are thereby saying that the determination of ultimacy, of good and evil, law and morality, is theirs to determine. This is another way of affirming their own deity.

Later on, Manfred makes an amazing statement, given the incipient existentialism of Byron's thinking. The existentialist affirms the sole reality of the moment, but Manfred, in the soliloquy that begins with the words, "We are the fools of time

---

6. *Ibid.*, III, CXIII.
7. "Manfred," Act II, scene I, ll. 38-41.

and terror," declares, "In life there is no present." The past and the future are implicitly denied, but why the present? Manfred, more radical than Jean-Paul Sartre, was a disengagement from all time. His existential moment is timeless. His answer to his dilemma is to declare himself *outside* of time and to welcome death: "my nature was averse to life." (Act III, scene I.) He declares that his own mind makes "requital for its good or evil thoughts," and the mind "is immortal." Therefore "tis not so difficult to die." The naturally immortal mind is outside the scope of God's law and its time-related judgments.

Similarly, in "Sardanapalus" that emperor disassociates himself from time and also declares, "I feel no penitence; my life is love." Time is the area of consequence, the arena for the outworkings of law. By renouncing time, Byron was separating the Romantic hero from law and history. God moves inexorably in time and history, so that judgment becomes inescapable. The Romantic representation of history is as tragedy. The revolutionist hopes to overcome and end history in a final world order without change. Byron saw time very often as defeat. Time means aging, death, law, and judgment. Cain, in "Cain: A Mystery," says "I have naught to ask," and also nothing to be thoughtful for. Cain tells Lucifer,

> I live,
> But live to die: and, living, see no thing
> To make death hateful, save an innate clinging,
> A loathsome, and yet all invincible
> Instinct of life, which I abhor, as I
> Despise myself, yet cannot overcome—
> And so I live. Would I had never lived!

The war against God becomes, as with the Marquis de Sade, a war against life. God's law is the way of life (Psalm 1) so that to war against God means in practice a war against morality and life.

In a study of the American novel, which, while not mentioning Romanticism, is in essence a study of it, Edwin T. Bowden analyzed *The Dungeon of the Heart, Human Isolation and the American Novel* (1961). The Romantic writer, having renounced God, man, and life, is imprisoned in his own being. He lives in a world without forgiveness. Instead of community, there is isolation and an anarchic individualism. Isolation is both sought and feared, idealized and yet seen as a tragic destiny. An identification with criminals ensues because the chosen isolation is from God and from the Christian community. The isolation and the solitude are from both God and man, certainly from the family. The family means responsibility; it means that priority does not belong to the individual but to the key community, and this, to the Romantic, is anathema. No Romantic ever saw the family as his happy home and setting! In writers like Thomas Wolfe, we see a "continual self-pity," a mark of the Romantic.[8] Together with this self-pity goes alienation and isolation. "One of the horrors of evil is that it prevents any real communication of man with man."[9] Its only antidote is escape, the isolated man seeks some kind of substitute for community. Self-pity prevents any resolution of the Romantic hero's problem. The escape into the revolutionary community, which Bowden sees as a tentative hope, is no hope at all. There is no escape from the dungeon of the heart because it is a prison man always carries with him.

Mario Praz, in his study, *The Romantic Agony* (1933), called attention to the reversal of the moral order by Shelley, in "The Revolt of Islam." God becomes the evil one who delights in the horror of the Fall.

> Thus evil triumphed, and the Spirit of evil,
> One Power of many shapes which none many know,
> One Shape of many names; the Fiend did revel
> In victory, reigning o'er a world of woe,
> For the new race of men went to and fro,
> Famished and homeless, loathed and loathing, wild,
> And hating good—for his immortal foe,
> He changed from starry shape, beauteous and mild,

8. Edwin T. Bowden, *The Dungeon of the Heart, Human Isolation and the American Novel* (New York, N.Y.: Macmillan, 1961), 69.

9. *Ibid.*, 771.

To a dire Snake, with man and beast unreconciled.[10]

For Shelley, "the serpent is the symbol of Good oppressed by Evil."[11]

Byron cultivated the image of the rebel, and who most represents the authority to rebel against than God? As we have seen, in "Lara" Byron described the heroic rebel as possessing "a vital scorn for all." (Canto I, XVII.) In "The Corsair" and "The Giaour," we see the same characteristic. Instead of morality and a commanding application of it to life, we have scorn and contempt as the marks of greatness. The Satanic smile and hints of secret-evils now mark the hero. Doom and gloom are for the Romantics marks of greatness, they identify the hero who defies God and man. In Byron's *Giaour*, we see mention of vampires and vampirism become a part of Romantic literature. Life is seen as haunted and full of evils. Man's destiny is a fatal one because God is the enemy of "free" man, meaning lawless man. Byron acted as though knowledge of his incest with Augusta gave him public validation; it was a "secret" he tried hard *not* to keep. He was determined to give people more than a hint that he was a Sadean man. To be damned was for Byron an aristocratic privilege. For him, the redeemed of God were the dregs of history. Mario Praz saw Byron and Swinburne as Satanists.[12]

Algernon Charles Swinburne (1837-1909) made clear that his primary inspiration came from the Marquis de Sade rather than Lord Byron.[13] Swinburne, a homosexual, hated God and replaced Him with man. In his "Chorus from *Atlanta in Clydon*," Swinburne spoke of "the holy spirit" of man. In his "Hymn to Proserpine," Swinburne wrote,

> Thou has conquered, O Galilean; the world has grown grey from thy breath;

---

10. Percy Bysshe Shelley, in *Complete Poems of Keats and Shelley*, "The Revolt of Islam," Canto I, XXVII; 40f.

11. Mario Praz, *The Romantic Agony* (New York, N.Y.: Meridian Books, 1933,1956), 83.

12. *Ibid.*, 267.

13. *Ibid.*, 215, 222-225, 232f., 278f.

> We have drunken of things Lethean, and fed on the fullness, of death.

For Swinburne, Christianity was the great disaster and evil of history:

> Though before thee the throned Cytherean be fallen, and hidden her head,
> Yet thy kingdom shall pass, Galilean, thy dead shall go down to thee dead.

Swinburne's poetry is like a bowl of sugar as one's dinner. It is self-consciously poetic, and it cloys and disgusts. His anti-Christianity was what Praz called Swinburne's "holy insurrection (the rebellion of man against God, thanks to which man will become god on earth."[14] Like Sade, Swinburne saw and held that "crime is Nature's law," and God is "a Being of supreme wickedness."[15]

Romanticism has seen the triumph of the homosexual in literature, music, art, and other fields. This is a logical development. St. Paul in Romans 1:22-23 tells us that homosexuality is the ultimate expression of man's revolt against God and the *burning out* of man. (In v. 27, *burned* is more accurately *burned out.*)

That burning out entails a hatred of God and man and a self-willed isolation. Byron addressed a poem, "Lines," to "The Rev. J.T. Becker, on his Advising the Author to Mix More with Society." Byron began his poem thus:

> Dear Becker, you tell me to mix more with mankind;
> I cannot deny such a precept is wise;
> But retirement accords with the tone of my mind:
> I will not descend to a world I despise.

But Byron was immensely popular with the reading public. He was a very popular figure and highly successful, and he played to his public. His contempt for mankind was a pose. How could he play the part of a lonely Romantic hero, misunderstood and abused, if he responded to the plaudits of

14. *Ibid.*, 223.
15. *Ibid.*, 225.

mankind? In fact, he went out of his way to be repulsive to people, to violate rules of manners and decency as well as morals.

It was imperative to view people with contempt. This came out in his brief poem, "John Keats:"

> Who kill'd John Keats?
> 'I,' says the Quarterly,
> So savage and Tartarly;
> "'Twas one of my feats.'
>
> Who shot the arrow?
> 'The poet – priest Milman
> (So ready to kill man),
> 'Or Southey, or Barrow.'

Keats (1795-1821) died of tuberculosis in Italy. The Romantics knew this, but they preferred to believe that it was his critics who killed Keats, and they freely slandered all who to any degree had been critical of Keats. Byron cited three names. The first was Henry Hart Milman, dean of St. Paul's after 1849, a professor of poetry at Oxford earlier, and the author of the excellent *History of Latin Christianity* (1854-55). Milman was a scholar of note. The second, Robert Southey (1774-1843), was Poet-Laureate after 1813. He was a writer for the *Quarterly Review.* These two men were both detested by Byron, and the death of Keats gave him an opportunity to blacken their names.

On top of that, the Romantic belief that their solitary souls were victims of the "hostile" mob was very important to them. The Romantics were Champions of victimhood, a stance which has now descended to "the masses." Homosexuals, lesbians, many blacks, leftists, artists, and many, many others see themselves as victims. The Romantics made of the peoples of the Twentieth Century a world of victims. Not until the evil influence of such thinking is broken will the Twenty-first Century see a rebirth of freedom. The champions of victimhood manifest an ability to create conflict and disaster.

Chapter 10

Karl Marx

Karl Marx (1818-1883) was very much in the tradition of Kant and Hegel. With Kant, he saw the real world as that which the philosophical radical saw it to be, the world within the rational mind. For Hegel, therefore, the rational is the real. Marx took this a step further: "The philosophers have only *interpreted* the world differently, the point is, to *change* it."[1] Interpretation means the attempt to understand a given thing, something created and established; to change the world means for Marx to give a new, man-made meaning. Instead of being content with a world that is, we must remake it into the new world order made in the image of man the rebel.

In the 1930s, in my student days, I was eager to learn what the world of thought had to say, past and present. I read through the classical writers of Greek and Rome, the philosophers of Europe, old and new, and also Karl Marx. Since I can no longer locate the two volumes of *Das Kapital* I once owned, I must have sold them, or else given them away. I had found them very confused and irrational. I discussed

---

1. Karl Marx, "Theses on Feuerbach," in Karl Marx and Friedrich Engels, *The German Ideology, Part I & II* (New York, N.Y.: International Publishers, 1947, 1960), 199.

them once with a friend, a very able student, from an Eastern Jewish family. Always an honest and telling analyst, he told me this: Marx is indeed what you say, an illogical, angry, and contradictory thinker. His "greatness" is not that he is a good thinker but in his unswerving insistence on *scientific* socialism. This means he rejects any *given*, any pre-existing meaning or assumption. For Marx, reality and the economy must be what man makes it. The "romantic" socialism Marx denounced insisted still on seeing some kind of given reality in the market. Marx essentially saw no reality other than a man-made one. This was his success. *Scientific* for Marx means man-made, not God-given.

Marx and Engels did refer often to *economic facts*. In this, they followed traditional economics. They were not interested in following the logical positions of the Young Hegelians. As Marx wrote, in the "Preface" to *The German Ideology*,

> Hitherto men have constantly made up for themselves false conceptions about themselves, about what they are and what they ought to be. They have arranged their relationships according to their ideas of God, of normal man, etc. The phantoms of their brains have gained the mastery over them. They, the creators, have bowed down before their creatures. Let us liberate them from the chimeras, the ideas, dogmas, imaginary beings under the yoke of which they are pining away. Let us revolt against the rule of thoughts. Let us teach men, says one (Ludwig Feuerbach), to exchange these imaginations for thoughts which correspond to the essence of man; says the second (Bruno Bauer), to take up a critical attitude to them; says the third Max Stirner, to knock them out of their heads; and — existing reality with collapse.[2]

The Kantian absorption with thought was not for Marx. He was fully in acceptance of Kant and Hegel; he wanted to shift the focus from thought about the world to action, to thought to change the world. He ridiculed the philosophical quest in the concluding paragraph of his "Preface."

---

2. Karl Marx, Preface to *The German Ideology*, in *ibid.*, 1.

> Once upon a time an honest fellow had the idea that men were drowned in water only because they were possessed with the idea of gravity. If they were to knock this idea out of their heads, say by stating it to be a superstition, a religious idea, they would be sublimely proof against any danger from water. His whole life long he fought against the illusion of gravity, of whose harmful results all statistics brought him new and revolutionary philosophers in German.[3]

The philosophers sought to *prove* that there is no God, and no God-created universe. Marx dismissed God, or the God-idea, as irrelevant. His task was to outline how the world can be remade by man. The working-creator had to be scientific man.

Richard Wurmbrand has cited evidence of Karl Marx's early Satanist ideas.[4] It is clear that his was a radical revolt against God. Like the Death of God school of thought of the early 1970's, he assumed, not the actual non-existence of God, but His irrelevance to man and history. His goal was the creation of an anti-God world, the creating of a totally man-made and man-ruled social order. He was thus contemptuous of the atheists of his day. Their absorption with ideas was absurd; they should be creating a world without God. The Hegelian philosophers ascribed to ideas an independent existence. Marx wanted to give the whole man an existence independent both of God and the philosophers. Man lives because of his economic activity; this gives him the means of subsistence. Hence, the independence of man must be sought by means of economics. This independence is not simply from capitalistic men, but from God. In Marx's words,

> Morality, religion, metaphysics, all the rest of ideology and their corresponding forms of consciousness, thus no longer retain the semblance of independence. They have no history, no development; but men, developing their material production and their material intercourse, alter, along with this their real existence, their thinking and the

3. *Ibid.*, 2.
4. Richard Wurmbrand, *Was Karl Marx a Satanist?* (Diane Books, 1976).

> products of their thinking. Life is not determined by consciousness, but consciousness by life.[5]

This is why economics was so important to Marx; the necessary success of his thinking would find vindication there. But Marx, usually as clear in his writing as a man can be, was very unclear in his economics. For all his emphasis on economics, it was there that his failure was so apparent and his thinking remarkably muddled. Man *must* be the creator essentially in the sphere of economics.

Economics, to be triumphant in the Marxist sense, should eliminate alienation and a consciousness of the self. The scientific socialist world order would be man-made, but men in it would be like the ants in an anthill. The ants and bees do not know a God; where man's alienation is ended neither will he.

Although economics is the heart of life, until now, Marx said revolutions have had political and other motive forces:

> (3) In all revolutions up till now the mode of activity always remained unscathed and it was only a question of a different distribution of this activity, a new distribution of labour to other persons, whilst the communistic revolution is directed against the preceding *mode* of activity, does away with *labour,* and abolishes the rule of all classes with the classes themselves, because it is carried through by the class which no longer counts as a class in society, is not recognized as a class, and is in itself the expression of the dissolution of all classes, nationalities, etc., within present society; and (4) Both for the production on a mass scale of this communist consciousness, and for the success of the cause itself, the alteration which can only take place in a practical movement, a *revolution*; this revolution is necessary, therefore, not only because the ruling class cannot be overthrown in any other way, but also because the class *overthrowing it* can only in a revolution succeed in ridding itself of all the muck of ages and become fitted to found society anew.[6]

---

5. *Ibid.*, "The German Ideology, Feuerbach, Opposition of the Materialistic and Idealistic Outlook," 14f.

6. *Ibid.*, 69.

Revolution is the Marxist pentecost; it is the means to the mass conversion of the peoples. This conversion, however, is downward. It is power from below, not power from above.

In the rest of *The German Ideology,* Marx denounces the socialists of his day who insist on a moral meaning to man's history and to socialism. Marx rejects all such attempts. "Scientific" means for Marx non-moral and non-theological.

For this reason; atheism was more than a peripheral belief for Karl Marx: it was essential to his system. *A priori*, there could be no God nor a prescribed good and evil from above. With the Prometheus of Aueschylus' *Prometheus Bound*, he could say, "In south all gods I hate."[7] For Marx, "Prometheus is the noblest of saints and martyrs in the calendar of philosophy."[8] So important was atheism to Karl Marx that he could write, "For Germany the *criticism of religion* is in the main complete, and criticism of religion is the premise of all criticism."[9] For Marx, man finds in the heavens and the gods only a reflection of himself. Man is not outside nor above the world, an aspect of nature. Truth is not *beyond* the world but, rather the world is the only truth there is. As a result, the intellectual's critique must be directed against the world and against politics. But basic to criticism in any sphere is atheism.

As a result, not only criticism in the philosophical sense, i.e., revolution in the intellectual sphere, but physical revolution, criticism in the political sphere, are necessary for Marx. In his "Contribution to the Critique of Hegel: Philosophy of Right," Marx saw Germany in need of both a radical critique of religion, and a revolutionary critique of its politics. This meant a radical secularization of society. This required a dissolution of both the existing states and churches, the negation of private property, and "the *dissolution of the hereto existing order* by the

---

7. Karl Marx, in the "Philosophy of Democritus and Philosophy of Epicurus, 1841, in K. Marx and F. Engels, *On Religion* (Moscow, U.S.S.R.: Foreign Languages Publishing House, 1955), 15.

8. *Idem.*

9. *Ibid.*, "Contribution to the Critique of Hegel's Philosophy of Right," 41.

proletariat."[10] Marx saw this revolution as one proclaiming "man to be the highest essence of man."[11] In other words, man cannot be defined by anything outside of, or beyond, himself. There is neither good nor evil, law nor morality, outside of man.

What the Marquis de Sade, and also Max Stirner, had affirmed on the purely personal sphere, Karl Marx affirmed on the political sphere. Man is beyond good and evil because there's nothing above, over, or beyond man other than man as a proletarian people.

In the *Communist Manifesto*, Marx and Engels called for the total re-organization of mankind in terms of a total statist control of every sphere.[12] For Marx, the old order had been essentially Christian. However much Marx at times saw this as a strictly controlled order, he was also aware of the extensive freedom it allowed. The old order, as a religious organization of society, depended on belief, on faith, whereas Marx's proposed order, as a statist one, would have to rely on coercion:

> The Communists disdain to conceal their views and aims. They openly declare that their ends can be attained only by the forcible overthrow of all existing social conditions. Let the ruling classes tremble at a Communistic revolution. The proletarians have nothing to lose but their chains. They have a world to win.
>
> Working men of all countries, unite![13]

This issue was between revelation and revolution. What was the source of value, God or man's labor? This was the essential question raised by the builders of the Tower of Babel. Like Marx, they were sure of the answer.

---

10. *Ibid.*, "Contribution to the Critique of Hegel's Philosophy of Right," 57.
11. *Ibid.*, 58.
12. Max Eastman, *Capital, The Communist Manifesto and Other Writings of Karl Marx* (New York, N.Y.: Carlton House, 1932), 342f.
13. *Ibid.*, 355.

Chapter 11

Persona

The word *person* has a curious history. It comes from the Etruscan *phersu*, into the Latin *persona*, meaning a *mask*. It had reference in both cases to the mask worn by actors, thus to a pretended character, a dramatic figure rather than a reality.

This use of *persona* pointed to a fact in classical antiquity, i.e., the insubstantial nature of man. Men were defined socially, by nation and by class. The view of classical antiquity with respect to people was in a sense closer to Karl Marx than to the Bible.

Plutarch's *Lives of the Noble Grecians and Romans* gives us examples of this, taken from the highest levels of society. Thus, we are told of Lycurgus of Sparta,

> Lycurgus allowed a man who was advanced in years and had a young wife to recommend some virtuous and approved young man, that she might have a child by him, who might inherit the good qualities of the father, and be a son to himself. On the other side, an honest man who had love for a married woman upon account of her modesty and the well-favoredness of her children, might, without formality, beg her company of her husband, that he might raise, as it were, from this plot of good ground, worthy and well-allied children for himself. And indeed, Lycurgus was of a persuasion that children were not so

> much the property of their parents as of the whole commonwealth, and, therefore, would not have his citizens begot of the first-comers, but by the best men that could be found; the laws of other nations seemed to him very absurd and inconsistent, where people would be so solicitous for their dogs and horses as to exert interest and to pay money to procure fine breeding, and yet kept their wives shut up, to be made mothers only by themselves, who might be foolish, infirm or diseased; as if it were not apparent that children of a bad breed would prove their bad qualities first upon those who kept and were rearing them, and well-born children, in like manner, their good qualities. These regulations, founded on natural and social grounds, were certainly so far from that scandalous liberty which was afterward charged upon their women, that they knew not what adultery meant.[1]

Some might object to this and maintain that the Athenians were not given to the practices of Sparta. In answer to this, one need only examine Plato's *Republic* and its belief that the philosopher-kings should have access to all women.

Turning to the Romans, Plutarch reported of Cato the Younger:

> It is thus related by Thrasea, who refers to the authority of Munatius, Cato's friend and constant companion. Among many that loved and admired Cato, some were more remarkable and conspicuous than others. Of these was Quintus Hortensius, a man of high repute and approved virtue, who desired not only to live in friendship and familiarity with Cato, but also to unite his whole house and family with him by some sort or other of alliance in marriage. Therefore he set himself to persuade Cato that his daughter Porcia, who was already married to Bibulus, and had borne him two children, might nevertheless be given to him, as a fair plot of land, to bear fruit also for him. "For," said he, "though this in the opinion of many men may seem strange, yet in nature it is honest, and profitable for the public, that a woman in the prime of her youth should not lie useless, and lose the fruit of her

---

1. Plutarch, *The Lives of the Noble Grecians and Romans* (New York, N.Y.: The Modern Library, n.d.), 61.

> womb, nor, on the other side, should burden and impoverish one man, by bringing him too many children. Also by this communication of families upon worthy men, virtue would increase, and be diffused through their posterity, and the commonwealth would be united and cemented by their alliances." Yet if Bibulous would not part with his wife altogether, he would restore her as soon as she had brought him a child, whereby he might be united to both their families. Cato answered that he loved Hortensius very well, and much approved of uniting their houses, but he thought it strange to speak of marrying his daughter, when she was already given to another. Then Hortensius, turning the discourse, did not hesitate to speak openly and ask for Cato's own wife, for she was young and fruitful, and he had already children enough. Nor can it be thought that Hortensius did this, as imagining Cato did not care for Marcia; for, it is said, she was then with request, but said that Philippus, the father of Marcia, ought to be also consulted. Philippus, therefore, being sent for, came; and finding they were well agreed, gave his daughter Marcia to Hortensius in the presence of Cato, who himself also assisted at the marriage. This was done at a later time, but since I was speaking of women, I thought it well to mention it now.[2]

Such a step was not commonplace, but it was logical, given the presuppositions of the classical view of man. It was a view widely present in the pre-Christian world, apart from the Hebrews. In Henri Frankfort's *Before Philosophy* (1946), John A. Wilson and Thorkild Jacobsen called attention to the fact that the cosmos was viewed in some cultures as a state, with both the gods and men sharing a continuity of being. The implication of this was that a stateless man was in effect a non-person. Man was defined by his place in this cosmic state.

For Biblical faith, however, man, having been created in the image of God (Gen. 1:26-28), is defined by that image, not by the cosmic state. That image of God in man is knowledge, righteousness or justice, holiness, and dominion (Gen. 1:26-28; Col. 3:10; Eph. 4:24). Man is thus under God and His law.

---

2. *Ibid.*, 932.

For non-Christian man, the universe is one continuous being, with gradations of being but no law from above. Cato the Younger, like Lycurgus' rules, decided the use of his wife in terms of humanistic ideas. Any Christian or Hebrew would have been governed by God's law.

In either case, the concept of the person differs. For the Roman, a person, philosophically, is a mask a *being* wears at a particular point in time and space. For Biblical faith, a person is a creature of God, created in His image, and subject to His laws.

For the modern humanist, a man can choose his lifestyle in terms of his preferences because no divine law can stand over him nor govern him. He sees himself as, philosophically, an evolutionary product, coming from below, and as a brief *persona* or mask worn by life and evolution. Because he wants freedom for his *persona*, he wants respect for the total environment, including rats, mice and cockroaches. His environmental regulations protect them: they are manifestations of *Gaia*, mother earth.

The early Church took the word *persona* and defined it, not as a mask on an actor, but in terms of *hypostasis* (from *hypo*, under, and *histemi*, to stand). There is one nature (*phusis*), one substance (*ousia*) to the Godhead and three persons. One of the greatest intellectual revolutions in the history of thought had taken place. People were no longer seen as temporary masks of being; persons now were creatures made in the *communicable* attributes of the triune God. A wife or daughter could no longer be legitimately disposed of at will; the law of God was now the source of government over all things.

This was a revolution in thinking that set the Christians against the world. Previously, this reference of all things to a supernatural order had been the mark of a "troublesome" people whom the Romans disliked and found "pestilential". Now the Christians far exceeded the Jews in their challenge to classical thought.

The primary reference of *persona* was now to God, three persons, Father, Son, and Holy Ghost. On the created level, man alone possesses personhood or personality in a created and derivative sense, derived from God's creative act.

In Hebrews 1:3, "the express image of his *person*" is in the Greek, *hypostasis*, substance or person. Another Greek word to express the Latin *persona* was *prosopon*, used in 2 Corinthians 4:6, "the glory of God in the *face* of Jesus Christ." Almost at once the New Testament was using Greek words (and, by implication, Latin) to express Biblical concepts. (There were, later, disputes between the Greek and Latin churches as to which word, *hypostasis* or *persona* was more accurate.)

Because of this changed meaning, *person* could no longer mean a mask or an appearance, a temporary expression of things in the stream of life, but rather stood for an act of God, a creature with a calling from God and an eternal destiny, a life in heaven or hell.

Being a *person* in the Christian sense thus meant a great responsibility, and an accountability to God. The new meaning began in the eternal being of the triune God rather than in an accident of evolution (a Greek concept in origin).

As Christianity grew, spread, and prevailed to some degree over Europe, and then in various parts of the world, attempts at re-definition set in. Sadly, some of the redefinition occurred within the Church. For example, L.W. Geddes, in *The Catholic Encyclopedia*, defined *personality* in terms of the concept of the self, without reference to God.[3] Centuries earlier, the Church's position had been clearer. The psychological definitions, Catholic and Protestant, were definitions downward, a retreat from the Biblical faith.

Besides the many psychological definitions, there were others, political, sociological, and, in the case of Karl Marx, economical. All these depersonalized man; instead of regarding

3. L.W. Geddes, "Personality," in *The Catholic Encyclopedia*, vol. 11 (New York, N.Y.: *The Encyclopedia Press*, 1911, 1913), 727-729.

himself as one created in the image of God; man now saw himself in terms of a Darwinian biology, a Marxist economics, a Freudian psychology, and so on. In all cases, the result was a diminished and emasculated man. Man was being remade into an emotional and psychological eunuch. Both man and history were depersonalized.

Karl Marx was important in this depersonalization. For him, economics was the determinative in the making of man, and man's remaking or regeneration would come by economics, by a revolution to create a communist world.

As a consequence of this depersonalization of man, and as a result of seeing man as an economic rather than a religious creature, Marx was hateful and venomous in his attitude towards Judaism and Christianity. In various essays, he attacked Christianity. In the essays of *A World Without Jews*, he vented his savage hatred of Jews. Both Jews and Christians should abandon their religion and seek, as the ground of human unity, *science*.[4] Marx wanted a state "professing no religion except its own statehood."[5] Because for Marx the definition of man did not come from God, his idea of society actually was closer to the anthill and the beehive. The end of alienation for him meant the end of personhood. Man would again be like the animals. Walt Whitman expressed this ideal very clearly:

> I think I could turn and live with animals, they are so placid and self-contain'd;
> I stand and look at them long and long.
> They do not sweat and whine about their condition;
> They do not lie awake in the dark and weep for their sins;
> They do not make me sick discussing their duty to God;
> No one is dissatisfied — not one is demented with the mania of owning things;
> Not one kneels to another, nor to his kind that lived thousands of years ago;

---

4. Karl Marx, *A World Without Jews* (New York, N.Y.: Philosophical Library, 1959), 3.

5. *Ibid.*, 9.

> Not one is respectable or industrious over the whole earth.[6]

Whitman was a city-man; he did not know wild animals. What he is obviously describing are cows, domestic animals cared for by man. And his longing is for the end of personhood.

As men today move in terms of Marx and Whitman, what we see is not the realization of a dream-world, but a reversion to paganism, to barbarism, and to new depths of savagery.

---

6. Walt Whitman, *Leaves of Grass*, "Walt Whitman," 32.

Chapter 12

Walt Whitman, The Artificial Man

Walt Whitman (1819-1892) was, like Nietzsche, an Emersonian, and, like Nietzsche, he *openly* developed the implications of Ralph Waldo Emerson (1803-1882) to their logical conclusions. Emerson, one of America's most subversive writers, wrote deceptively, as a prophet of the good American life, so that his appeal was to men as diverse as Nietzsche on the one hand, and Robert Welch, founder of the John Birch Society, on the other.

Walt (originally Walter) Whitman was an urban man, mainly associated with printing and journalism before he assumed the mantle of America's prophet, the prophet of democracy and the voice of cosmic consciousness. Richard Maurice Buck, in *Cosmic Consciousness*, saw Walt Whitman as "the best, most perfect example the world has so far had of the Cosmic Sense." Whitman was a self-manufactured man. As Esther Shephard demonstrated, Whitman patterned himself after fictional concepts of the untutored natural prophet who spouts pure poetry and truth, an idea derived from George Sand's novels, and from others.[1] When Shephard's book was

[1] Esther Shephard, *Walt Whitman's Pose* (New York, N.Y.: Harcourt, Brace, 1936, 1938).

published, I was a university student. I asked a professor about it and was told that the book was meaningless and irrelevant. Only later did it occur to me that both the professor and Whitman were homosexuals and had a common stake in pretension. The only honest note in Whitman's writings was the homosexual one, and he avoided probings on that.

As the prophet of full democracy, Whitman could not allow for distinctions and moral judgments, and his poems are a long praise of the total acceptance of everything — except Christianity. His poems do poorly as poetry; they are read as a substitute Bible, and some were set to solemn, hymn-like music. Whitman wanted a liberty for all things and practices which are non-Christian. He insisted that the true meaning of democracy and America is the liberation from morality. His long poem, "Walt Whitman," is an egocentric celebration of his prophetic "calling." He went so far as to have a photograph taken of himself as Christ, "The Christ Picture."[2] His poem "Walt Whitman" also celebrates pantheism, of which he is the prophet and voice:

> I celebrate myself;
> And what I assume you shall assume;
> For every atom belonging to me, as good belongs to you.[3]

Whitman insisted on the goodness of all things: "Clear and sweet is my Soul, and clear and sweet is all that is not my Soul."[4] The equality of everything was assured, together with faith in himself:

> I believe in you, my Soul — the other I am must not abase itself to you;
> And you must not be abased to the other.[5]

Whitman asserted the radical equality of all things: we are "lucky" to live and "just as lucky to die."[6] No moral judgments

---

2. *Ibid.*, opposite 52.
3. Walt Whitman, *Leaves of Grass*, "Walt Whitman," 1 (New York, N.Y.: Grosset & Dunlap, n.d.), 5.
4. *Ibid.*, 7; 3.
5. *Ibid.*, 9; 5.
6. *Ibid.*, 12; 7.

can stand, nor biological ones: all things are equally valid in a pantheistic universe. He declared himself to be "the caresser of life,"[7] but he was, in terms of his premises, also the caresser of murder, rape, and death. All are equal to him, the deacon, the farm boy, and the prostitute. In fact, in 1860, he wrote "To a Common Prostitute,"

> Be composed — be at ease with me — I am Walt Whitman, liberal and lusty as Nature;
> Not till the sun excludes you, do I exclude you;
> Not till the waters refuse to glisten for you, and the leaves to rustle for you, do my words refuse to glisten and rustle for you.
>
> My girl, I appoint with you an appointment — and I charge you that you make preparation to be worthy to meet me,
> And I charge you that you be patient and perfect till I come.
>
> Till then, I salute you with a significant look that you do not forget me.[8]

Prophet Whitman saw himself as an elemental force, as a kind of incarnation of Nature. Normally not given to distinctions, he here demands that the girl "make preparation to be worthy to meet me." And what could that be? Our Nature prophet does not say!

Whitman addresses Jesus Christ as a "dear brother" (in "To Him that was Crucified") and as one whom Whitman understood, although Jesus' followers did not. He declared Jesus to be like himself, above all choosing of sides and beyond all insistence on moral judgments:

> I specify you with joy, O my comrade, to salute you, and to salute those who are with you, before and since — and those to come also.
> That we all labor together, transmitting the same charge and succession;
> We few, equals, indifferent of lands, indifferent of times;

7. *Ibid.*, 17; 13.
8. *Ibid.*, 319.

We, encloser of all continents, all castes — allowers of all theologies,
Compassionates, perceivers, rapport of men,
We walk silent among disputes and assertions, but reject not the disputers, nor anything that is asserted;
We hear the bawling and din — we are reach'd by divisions, jealousies, recriminations on every side,
They close peremptorily upon us, to surround us, my comrade,
Yet we walk unheld, free, the whole earth over, journeying up and down, till we make our ineffaceable mark upon time and the diverse eras,
Till we saturate time and eras, that the men and women of races, ages to come, may prove brethren and lovers, as we are.[9]

The falsity and idiocy of this is readily apparent. Whitman asserts his equality with Christ and sees Christ as rejecting all theologies and moral divisions. All men are to be, according to this common faith, "brethren and lovers, as we are," which to Whitman meant fellow homosexuals. Whitman passed as a poet, but was closer to being a self-made madman! He was his own ultimate force:

Why should I pray? Why should I venerate and be ceremonious?
Having pried through the strata, analyzed to a hair, counsell'd with doctors, and calculated close,
I find no sweeter fat than sticks to my own bones.
In all people I see myself — none more, and not one a barley-corn less;
And the good or bad I say of myself, I say of them.[10]

He saw himself as the voice of the Kosmos, the voice of all peoples and all things, the voice of slaves, prostitutes, or criminals, of "forbidden voices," and of everything:

Divine am I inside and out, and I make holy whatever I touch or am touch'd from;
The scent of these arm-pits, aroma finer than prayer;
This head more than churches, bibles, and all the creeds.

---

9. *Ibid.*, 317f; dated 1860.
10. *Ibid.*, 26; "Walt Whitman," 20.

> If I worship one thing more than another, it shall be the spread of my own body, or any part of it.
> Translucent mould of me, it shall be you!
> Shaded ledges and rests, it shall be you!
> Firm masculine colter, it shall be you.[11]

A "colter" is a plow or a knife, and it was once used to refer to the penis, and Whitman tells us he worshipped his sexuality, and he found the smell of his arm-pits finer than prayer, bibles, and creeds. And why not — if he was indeed divine and holy? He did add, "O I am wonderful!" He is everyman, but he is more. All are equal in this pantheistic universe of Walt Whitman, but he is their incarnate voice.

In section 43 of "Walt Whitman," he tells the priests he does not despise them; he "accepts" Jesus (on his, Whitman's, terms). He, the voice of all, offers his benediction to all. In 46, he speaks to his "Spirit," capitalized like the Holy Spirit. In 48, he declares, "nothing, not God, is greater to one than one's self is."

Like Sade, Whitman abolished all moral law and distinctions. Unlike Sade, he held that the world beyond good and evil is somehow wonderful and holy. In his poem, "To Think of Time" (1855), Whitman saw all things as beneficent:

> What will be, will be well — for what is, is well,
> To take interest is well, and not to take interest shall be well.[12]

In Whitman's thinking, the world was beyond Biblical good and evil and therefore in a blissful Nirvana. Such thinking came from Emerson. Carlyle disliked it in his friend Emerson. According to Joseph Slater,

> In spite of genuine distaste, which became shock and moral indignation when they heard Emerson assert that even in a brothel man "is on his way to all that is great an good," the Carlyles continued to attend his lectures.[13]

---

11. *Ibid.*, 32; 24.
12. *Ibid.*, 87, 6.
13. Joseph Slater, editor, *The Correspondence of Emerson and Carlyle* (New York, N.Y.: Columbia University Press, 1964, 1965), 38f.

Sade's successors wanted God abolished and universal bliss to prevail. They wanted a lawless world to be seen as holy. Sade would perhaps have been both amused and appalled at the naïve nature of such people. If God goes, what remains? The world *and the mind of man* are His creation.

In "I Sing the Body Electric" (1895), Whitman rhapsodizes on the body as "sacred." He borrows the term from religion, trying to retain some meaning even as he rejects the origin. He can only burble because, having destroyed definition and demarcation, he has no criterion by which he can define anything. In "Great are the Myths" (1855), he reduces the Bible to myth, declares to be "Great" youth and old age, the Earth, Language, Justice, and Life, and more. But his pantheism and his equalization of all things makes his praise empty. Because he hails all things as equally valid, what difference does anything make? His concept of democracy negates all meaning. In "This Compost" (1856), Whitman celebrated the fact that all things die and rot to provide compost for what comes next. Is this any ground for meaning and joy that all things become fertilizer? Is this a ground for comfort and joy? Whitman's unending gush is no substitute for meaning. His frequent wide generalizations give us little content. In "A Woman Waits for Me" (1856), Whitman wrote:

> Sex contains all,
> Bodies, Souls, meanings, proofs, purities, delicacies, results, promulgations,
> Songs, commands, health, pride, the maternal mystery, the seminal milk;
> All hopes, benefactions, bestowals,
> All the passions, loves, beauties, delights of the earth,
> All the governments, judges, gods, follow'd persons of the earth,
> These are all contain'd in sex, as parts of itself, and justifications of itself.
> Without shame the man I like knows and avows the deliciousness of his sex,
> Without shame the woman I like knows and avows hers.[14]

[14] *Ibid.*, 198.

This childish spouting says little; it is pseudo-profound and inane. In what sense are all things, including governments and the world order "contain'd in sex, as parts of itself, and justifications of itself?" Do we know the world better by reducing it to sex, atoms, humors, or anything else?

In "Respondez!" (1856) Whitman called for the transvaluation of all standards:

> Let us all, without missing one, be exposed in public, naked, monthly, at the peril of our lives! Let our bodies be freely handled and examined by whoever chooses!
> Let nothing but copies at second hand be permitted to exist upon the earth!
> Let the earth desert God, nor let there ever henceforth be mention'd the name of God!
> Let there be no God![15]

Whitman was very prone to homosexual daydreams; he equated a surplus of words with poetry and profundity. He claimed, "I project the history of the future."[16] In "We Two — How Long We Were Fooled" (1860), Whitman expressed his usual self-identification with Nature, with plants, roots, grass, fish, hawks, with everything.[17] This identification was assumed to have a mystical harmony and joy. For Whitman, death and life were equal, as were all things else. In "Native Moments" (1860), he insisted that he loved "law" persons, prostitutes, and shunned persons.[18] He compared himself to Adam, walking naked early in the morning, and he invited others to touch and handle his "Body."[19] He was in his eyes an unfallen new Adam, here to save the world with his "gospel." He instructed "Recorders ages hence" on how to view him, a very flattering self-description of a "prophet" of love.[20]

In 1865, in "Chanting the Square Deific," Whitman acted as the voice of all things, Jehovah and Satan, Brahma, Saturn, the

---

15. *Ibid.*, 214; "Respondez!"
16. *Ibid.*, 233; "To a Historian," 1860.
17. *Ibid.*, 257.
18. *Ibid.*, 258.
19. *Ibid.*, 260; *Ibid.*, 260; "As Adam, Early in the Morning," 1860.
20. *Ibid.*, 269; "Recorders Ages Hence," 1860.

Holy Spirit, and "the general Soul."[21] The marriage of God and Satan is basic to the modern temper, because such a union reduces God from absolute ultimacy to being a facet of the totality, "the general Soul." This reduces morality in the Biblical sense to no more than one life-style among many, no more true or false than any other faith. The homosexual way of life is then as valid as any; the criminal is as good as the saint, and the whore is as good as the virgin. In fact, if the sodomite, the criminal, and the whore insist on the validity of their way, they then represent a higher awareness of "reality." Hence, Whitman's song was himself with all his vices.[22]

With the passing years, Whitman's verse became very repetitious; after all, pantheism allows for little else. His words became bathos, as witness "The Singer in the Prison" (1868).[23] In "A Clear Midnight" (1881), he echoes his old separation from books and scholarship and his "free flight into the wordless."[24] His pantheistic pseudo-mysticism required a flight from knowledge and meaning into gush and ecstasy over a cosmic and undifferentiated blob or mess.

Because men found a cosmic meaning hard to live with because it means law and judgment, responsibility and accountability, men found Whitman "great" because they wanted to join him in escaping from meaning.

Whitman had his imitators in abundance. In England, Edward Carpenter (1844-1929), an ex-clergyman in the Church of England, in *Towards Democracy*, gave to those who loved a non-judgmental, homo-erotic view of the world, as much gush as Whitman did, and in the same manner. Carpenter also saw himself as a prophet, a humanistic messiah. In "I Am a Voice," we are told,

> I am a voice singing the song of deliverance —
> Centuries long, centuries long, floating aloft in ecstasy.

---

21. *Ibid.*, 425-427.
22. *Ibid.*, 427; "One's-Self I Sing," 1867.
23. *Ibid.*, 448-451.
24. *Ibid.*, 536.

> Surprised at myself — to find myself looking out on this landscape here — to be engaged on these occupations and plans which people call mine, but which are not mine at all — to be living in this house which is nothing to me whether I live in it or not — to be fretting myself with these and these anxieties and cares — to be this limited and foolish mortal that I am;
>
> Yet again at intervals soaring aloft, going back again to my home in the sky,
> To sing for all time,
> The song of joy — of deliverance.[25]

An imitator like Carpenter was no small curse on Whitman!

But what of the churches? Where have they stood on Whitman and his radical democracy, on the equality of good and evil, God and Satan? Mostly, they have been silent. This has perhaps been preferable to their speaking. Thus, in the February 16, 1953 issue of *Monday Morning*, a magazine for the clergy of the Presbyterian Church, New York, a review of Arthur E. Briggs' book, *Walt Whitman, Thinker and Artist* appeared. The review, in full, said:

> I thoroughly agree with the author that Whitman's poetical gifts continued throughout his life, in contrast with some who contend that his genius declined before the Civil War. Personally, I have always been rather reluctant to psychoanalyze Whitman, I would rather accept him as the "good gray poet." Had I been a contemporary of Whitman, no doubt I would have been as shocked by his "barbaric yawp," his blatant egotism, and his offensive obscenities. However, he came to me full-orbed, years after his death, and I appreciate his poetic gifts. He, undoubtedly, was the 19th century prophet of the common man. I have always loved him for the golden haze of mysticism which pervades much of his poetry. I have admired him for his Homeric gift of choosing the right word or phrase. I have been captured by his serenity.
>
> I cannot agree with the author in classifying Whitman as "an ethical humanist." His belief in the personality of God

---

25. Edward Carpenter, *Towards Democracy* (New York, N.Y.: Albert & Charles Boni, 1922, 1935), 177.

> and the immorality of the soul surely places him "on the side of the angels." This is particularly true of his poems written after 1870. However, I am greatly indebted to the author for the many fine tributes which he gives to Whitman.[26]

No doubt such a pastor would have found redeeming qualities in the Marquis de Sade. His opinion to the contrary, Whitman was *not* an *ethical* humanist, but simply a *humanist* who affirmed the radical equality of all things.

Whitman and Dewey would appreciate the United States of the 1990s with its moral relativism and its equalitarian democratic goals.

In the world of the 1990s, equality is clearly affirmed. A father, about to spend a fortune educating his college-bound son, rather diffidently urged him to moral behavior. The son asked him, saying, "Dad, you have your standards, and I have mine, I respect your code, and you should respect mine." Democratic moral relativism is prevalent. A close friend called me yesterday. A playmate of his five-year old daughter decided she wanted to eat, and she demanded that her host family feed her. (It was not dinner time yet.) Another playmate, a boy, decided against going home when his father called. Instead of being ordered home, the father spent twenty minutes persuading the boy home would be best. This is equalitarianism and democracy, everyone's will as good as anyone's. Or, take the argument against orthodox Christianity by some homosexuals. They saw it as evil because it declared homosexuality and other practices to be sin, to be morally wrong. This was a violation of democracy.

More can be said, but the problem should be obvious by now. Edward Carpenter titled one poem, "Lo! What a World I Create," and he said he was creating it for "my own, my lovers."[27] Indeed, Carpenter and Whitman were creating a world for their lovers, and there would be no room in it for others.

---

26. H.S. Rambo, in *Monday Morning*, February 16, 1953.

27. Carpenter, *op. cit.*, 477.

Whitman was an artificial man, a fabrication of his own making. In his later years, he tried to claim that he had, indeed, been very much involved with women, rather unconvincingly so. He had created a mythical Walt Whitman, and as an old man Walter had trouble vindicating him. Very little about Whitman rang true. W.A. Orton said of Whitman,

> His (Whitman's) sensuality repels because it is not sensual enough; it is too impersonal, too cerebral, too much a part of his thin conceptual universe.[28]

Like his blowsy heartiness, all things about Whitman, other than his homosexuality, rang false. They were artificial, manufactured aspects of a prophetic pose. Whitman is well regarded wherever artificial man exists, and his fame will perish as synthetic facades collapse and artificial men receive the bored indifference they deserve.

---

[28]. William Aylott Orton, *America in Search of Culture* (Boston, Massachusetts: Little, Brown, 1933), 112.

Chapter 13

Non-Persons

History has seen many killers, political leaders who have murdered millions, and a variety of evildoers who have seen their fulfillment in criminal activities. To any such list we must add the philosophers whose ideas provided the impetus for human action. Ideas do have consequences, as Richard Weaver pointed out. In Genesis 11:1-9, we are told of the builders of the Tower of Babel that they sought to create a one-world order in defiance of, and without, God. A united mankind, they believed, could rival God and create its own order and law.

Babel failed, but the civil orders which followed defined man in terms of the State, so that to be a stateless man was to be a non-person. In his *Politics*, Aristotle defined the accepted wisdom of the ancient world. He held that "the state is a creation of nature, and that man is by nature a political animal."[1] In fact, said Aristotle, "man is more of a political animal than bees or any other gregarious animals." The state is "prior to the family and the individual." This is a basic premise for Aristotle. He wrote,

---

1. Aristotle, *Politics*, Book I, 2, 1253 (New York, N.Y.: The Modern Library, n.d.)

> The proof that the state is a creature of nature and prior to the individual is that the individual, when isolated, is not self-sufficing; and therefore he is like a part in relation to the whole. But he who is unable to live in society, or who has no need because he is sufficient for himself, must be either a beast or a god: he is no part of a state. A social instinct is implanted in all men by nature, and yet he who first founded the state was the greatest of benefactors. For man, when perfected, is the best of animals, but, when separated from law and justice, he is the worst of all; since armed injustice is the more dangerous, and he is equipped at birth with arms, meant to be used by intelligence and virtue, which he may use for the worst ends. Wherefore, if he have not virtue, he is the most unholy and the most savage of animals, and the most full of lust and gluttony. But justice is the bond of men in states, for the administration of justice, which is the determination of what is just, is the principle of order in political society.[2]

Now in his *Ethics*, Aristotle defines injustice as "all that is contrary to law."[3]

Thus, for Aristotle, the State defines man and the State defines justice. Law is created by the state, and statist law is justice. What this meant was that *the stateless man was a non-person.* The practical consequences we see in the Hittite laws. For example, incest was a capital crime. For a man to cohabit with his wife's sister or mother meant death *if they were free women.* If, however, a man engaged with sex with a slave girl and her mother, or if a father and son, or some free men did so, there was no offense and no punishment.[4] The same act meant incest and death where a free woman was involved, and yet meant nothing with slave women because they were non-persons. This was common to many cultures.

In Rome, according to Florence Dupont, sexual offenses had nothing to do with age or gender and "everything to do with

---

2. *Ibid.* Bk. I, 2, 1253, 55.
3. Aristotle, *Ethics*, Book V, chapt. 2, J.A.K. Thomson, translator (Harmondsworth, Middlesex, England: Penguin Books, 1953, 1958), 143.
4. Hittite Laws, in James B. Pritchard, editor, *Ancient Near Eastern Texts* (Princeton University Press: Princeton, New Jersey, 1950, 1955), 196.

legal status." Was the child or adult a slave and therefore a non-person, or a free person? Citizenship defined people. "Romans were social beings: they did not consider themselves human unless they belonged to some form of society."[5] In fact, Dupont states, "Citizens alone were possessed of souls. Children, slaves, and women were soulless bodies: their father, master or husband provided their *animus*."[6] In Rome's days of "virtue," sex outside marriage with a freeborn woman was forbidden. With slaves, non-persons, nothing was prohibited, and modern bans against perversions and incest did not apply to sex with Roman slaves. The slave-owner, as a free citizen, could copulate with his slaves, including those who were genetically his sons and daughters, and his sons did the same.[7] The slaves were legally non-persons, and therefore the act did not count. The only moral consideration exercised by the free man was this: Was he too prone to surrender to his instincts? What he did was not the important fact, but the degree of his enslavement to "his brutish instincts."[8] Sex with slave children was commonplace. It apparently also took place with free children, but efforts were made to prevent this.[9] But slaves, young and old, being non-persons, were casually used. A master could be fond of his slaves, but they were still non-persons before the law, and "citizens alone possessed a soul."

The early church came into the Roman world with a radically different faith. In terms of Scripture, it held that man is created in the image of God (Gen. 1:26-28), in knowledge, righteousness (or justice), holiness, and dominion (Gen. 1:27-28; Col. 3:10, Eph. 4:24). Paul on Mars' Hill declared:

> 24. God that made the world and all things therein, seeing that he is Lord of heaven and earth, dwelleth not in temples made with hands;

---

5. Florence Dupont, *Daily Life in Ancient Rome* (Oxford, England: Blackwell, (1989) 1992), 117, 9.
6. *Ibid.*, 10.
7. *Ibid.*, 118.
8. *Ibid.*
9. *Ibid.*, 226-228.

> 25. Neither is worshipped with men's hands, as though he needed any thing, seeing he giveth to all life, and breath, and all things,
> 26. And hath made of one blood all nations of men for to dwell on all the face of the earth, and hath determined the times before appointed, and the bounds of their habitation;
> 27. That they should seek the Lord, if haply they might feel after him, and find him, though he be not far from every one of us:
> 28. For in him we live, and move, and have our being; as certain also of your own poets have said, For we are also his offspring.
> 29. Forasmuch then as we are the offspring of God, we ought not to think that the Godhead is like unto gold, or silver, or stone graven by art and man's device.
> 30. And the times of this ignorance God winked at; but now commandeth all men every where to repent:
> 31. Because he hath appointed a day, in the which he will judge the world in righteousness by that man whom he hath ordained; whereof he hath given assurance unto all men, in that he hath raised him from the dead. (Acts 17:24-31).

It is helpful, in understanding this text, to realize that these key facts governed the Greeks to whom Paul spoke. First, Greek thought required a first cause, God, because it rejected an infinite regress. They needed God as a limiting concept, an idea rather than the sovereign Being. Second, the perfect God of Greek philosophy could not involve himself with creating or creation. He had to be too far above such activity to be even remotely involved. Aristotle thus formulated the theory of the eternity of the world.[10] Third, this answer was necessary because "for a Hellenistic Greek, no god could touch matter, and still remain god." The Christian doctrine of the incarnation was thus intensely offensive to the Greeks.[11]

---

10. Patrick Madigan, *Christian Revelation and the Completion of the Aristotelian Revolution* (Lanham, Maryland: University Press of America, 1988), 33.
11. *Ibid.*, 83.

With this in mind, Paul's carefully chosen words become more understandable. It was the inscription, "To the Unknown God," that led to Paul's words. First, Paul declares that God is the Creator. The universe had a beginning in God's creative act. He is both Creator and the ultimate Being who is beyond all human depiction. Having created man, and being beyond man, He can neither be depicted by man's art, nor worshipped in man's way.

Second, God is the Creator of all mankind, "of one blood," so that man is not defined by the State but by God, whose predestination determines the limits of men and nations.

Third, men are to worship God, who is close at hand, transcendent, yet omnipresent and immanent. We are God's creation, and He is our total environment, "for in him we live, and move, and have our being." Instead of being an object of knowledge, He is the only true ground of all knowledge. This means that we must rethink all our ways of knowing.

Fourth, having sent His Son, God is no longer indulgent of men's folly and ignorance. There will be, at the end of history, a day of accounting for all, a judgment day. The Judge will be God the Son, Jesus Christ, whom God the Father resurrected from the dead.

The implication of all this is that the State does not define man. Stateless persons are not non-persons. God is the definer because He is the Creator.

But modern man agrees with ancient man. He sees with Aristotle the State as the definer of persons and non-persons. This is because modern man, first, insists on seeing the state as the vessel of salvation. The State is seen as the problem solver and the benefactor. The State makes the laws, and the laws define man. At the same time, the flight from Christian morality has meant the rise of pornography. The people in pornographic writings (and films, magazines, etc.) are non-persons. They exist to provide fuel for the pornographic imagination. Darwinism has reduced man to a higher ape, and, in spite of all efforts to the contrary, the logical result has been the dehumanization of man. For some, the environment, as an entity to be worshipped and preserved, has taken priority over humanity. Education has furthered the depersonalization of men by stressing the environment unduly and by striking at morality as God's law prescribes it. The churches, by their antinomianism, having replaced God's law with the State's law, have foolishly allowed the State to be the defining power. In one state, in the 1970s, I learned of a number of "evangelical" churches, varying between 60 and 100 in their meetings, who were agreeable to state controls and laws whether of Christian schools, of questions of abortion and homosexuality, and soon, as long as they were free to proclaim John 3:16. But how long could the meaning of that text stand before a state claiming the prerogative of God in law-making?

The modern term for the major part of the peoples of the earth is "the masses." Marxists have not been alone in using this term. This is one of the many aspects of depersonalization.

The early Church rescued abandoned babies and reared them as Christians. They were technically and legally non-persons and hence slaves, but in the Christian community they were brothers and sisters in Christ. Some became in time pastors and bishops. The medieval era steadily eliminated slavery and the status of non-persons, but Renaissance humanism, with its revival of Greco-Roman ideas, brought back slavery, and the Enlightenment furthered it.

Modern statism and one-worldism seek to further the statist re-definition of man and the de-Christianization of society. This process is well on its way. The prelude to it was the massive saturation of education with classical culture. It is an ironic fact that men concentrate on Plato's philosopher-kings rather than the majority of the people in Plato's Republic.

In our urban streets, gangs of young killers see nothing wrong in killing others (seen as non-persons), while enraged at harm done to one of their own gang members. In all non-Christian thinking, *others* are depersonalized. For the faithful in Christ, the Great Commission requires their discipling into Christ's community, Kingdom and life (Matt. 28:18-20).

The news is full of reports and rumors of war, of murders, and of child-molestation. It is commonplace for people to be treated as non-persons. Ideas do have consequences.

Chapter 14

Being and Self-Definition

The concept of *being* has a curious history, and, now, a curious neglect, both by philosophy and theology. From the Greeks to the existentialists and on, it has been variously defined. The early Greek philosophers defined it in contrast to *change*, or *becoming*. True *being* is changeless and eternal, whereas *becoming* is changeable, illusory, and to some extent, unreal. Aristotle held that being is eternal in itself but its manifestations are in change.

The Milesians had held that *being* is the cosmic substance, timeless, spaceless, and undifferentiated. Nothing else has real existence. This could mean that man's life is lived in non-being. Aristotle resolved this by holding that, while material atoms are in, and basic to the world around us, their essence is the unfolding changing world around us; it is more than illusion: it is being in process. True being is thus an unfolding essence, and reality is in phenomena. The two are linked together. Only when the phenomena are fully and totally developed will the true being, the essence, be known. Thus, all knowledge, until then, is tentative. Form is continually becoming matter, and the answer awaits the *possible* completion of this process. All being is one continuous being, although many things in process have a thinness of being. God is pure form, and matter is pure possibility. Matter, like God, has always existed; how the two can inter-work Aristotle could not explain. This perspective has, with variations, dominated philosophy in the Western tradition.

Biblical Christianity has a very different perspective. Instead of one being, we have the uncreated Being of God, and then the created being of the entire world of creation. There can be no confusion between uncreated and created being. The Council of Chalcedon (451 A.D.), insisted on the perfect union without confusion of the two natures of Christ.

Too many thinkers, however, preferred the Greek answer, and the concept of the Great Chain of Being became popular, especially with the Enlightenment. Everything participated, in this theory, in the Being of God, but, the lower on the scale of creation, the thinner the participation in Being. All being, in this concept, is God-Being, but most things, as I heard a student in my youth lightly describe it, are lower in their "God-Stuff."

For Jean-Paul Sartre, the dualism of appearance and essence was illusory. The whole of *Being and Nothingness* was a confused effort to define being in terms of the Kantian, existentialist framework. The language of philosophy, its terminology and assumptions, Sartre dismissed as no longer valid. Since the existentialist movement is alone real, and since religious, social, and emotional data exist only in our consciousness for Sartre, the logic of his position meant that being is existential man, who is then his own god. In the process, however, all meaning was nihilated, so that no meaning remains, and *to be* is *nothingness.* The death of God becomes the death of meaning and of God.

The Death of God school of thought similarly found itself negating itself:

> For Altizer, modern culture and so any contemporary man who expresses its mood, finds the transcendent God both unreal and repressive, a threat to our human

> creativity, authenticity, and freedom; only, said he, if we dare to declare this transcendent God dead and cease to depend on him, can we appropriate the divine that is immanent in us in the Living Word that always changes its forms.[1]

This also leaves man as a self-definer in a world without meaning. The "Living Word" becomes whatever meaning it has at the will of the reader, so that meaning becomes subjective, ephemeral, and the creature of the moment. In Acts 17:28, St. Paul spoke of God as He in whom "we live, and move, and have our being." Many now deny this and replace God with *time*. But time from of old has been as much under attack as perhaps God. Parmenides (b. 515 B.C.), of the Eleatic school, identified Being as all that fills space; it is also timeless, and change and becoming are irrational illusions. Heraclitus (c. 536-470 B.C.) of Ephesus denied permanence and held that change is universal. He held, "All things are one."[2] For Parmenides, "Being has no coming-into-being and no destruction."[3] Without the triune God of Scripture, man has always had intellectual as well as moral problems, and the two have been inter-connected.

Where meaning is questioned, morality is questioned or denied. Where God is denied, all meaning soon disappears and philosophy becomes skepticism and cynicism. Wittgenstein's moral life was simply an expression of his philosophy. To raise questions about being is to question life.

Now all this is essentially related to our modern world. When men deny the Being who created all things, the triune God, they deny their own being. To assume that by billions of amazing miracles something evolved out of absolute nothingness is to abandon not only morality, but rationality, for immoralism and madness. As a student, I found, in a

---

1. Langdon Gilkey, "God, Idea of Since 1800," in Philip. Wiener, editor in chief, *Dictionary of the History of Ideas*, vol. 3 (New York, N.Y.: Charles Scribner's Sons, 1973), 364.

2. Kathleen Freeman, *Ancilla to the Pre-Socratic Philosophers* (Cambridge, Massachusetts: Harvard University Press, 1957), 28, no. 50.

3. *Ibid.*, 43; 7, 8.

discussion with a radically cynical and immoral student, that he was emphatic in his denial of God and meaning. He saw man only as an over-developed form of protoplasm and denied any and all responsibility to his parents and to the young woman he cynically used. By this means he prevented any and all considerations of morality and responsibility. He was insistent that man is no more than a copulating animal. While insistent on getting his "due" in money from his parents and part-time work, he denied the validity of any obligation, courtesy, or code of honor.

Since then, what he represented has become commonplace. The Christian view of being affirms the uncreated and eternal Being of the triune God, and the created being of man and all things else. The denial of this means a denial of law and power from above and its quest from below. *Being* becomes progressively an unacceptable category of thought because it has reference to meaning, and meaning is rejected together with God. The rejection of meaning becomes a passion. In the late 1970s, outside a chapel in Westwood, Los Angeles, where I then preached weekly, a student from the university came on the scene as the worshippers, after the service, were visiting. He started confronting people with obscenities and pornographic remarks about Christianity. The only reality, he insisted, was copulation, and Christians had too many "hang-ups" to enjoy it. There was no other meaning for him.

This is not surprising. *Meaning* has become a complicated thing in modern philosophy whose subject is often simply language, and its essential non-meaning! Max Black, in the *Dictionary of Philosophy*, called it "a highly ambiguous term."[4] The denial of God means at the least questioning both being and meaning. Dostoyevsky held that, if there is no God, then everything is permitted.

---

4. Max Black, "Meaning," in Dagobert D. Runes, editor, *Dictionary of Philosophy* (New York, N.Y.: Philosophical Library, 1960), 193.

In his novel, *The Possessed*, Dostoyevsky depicts Kirillov as a man determined to kill God. But this requires a strange conclusion:

> I can't understand how an atheist could know that there is no God and not kill himself on the spot. To recognize that there is no God and not to recognize at the same instant that one is God oneself is an absurdity, else one would certainly kill oneself. If you recognize it you are sovereign, and then you won't kill yourself but will live in the greatest glory. But one, the first, must kill himself, for else who will begin and prove it. Now I am only a god against my will and I am unhappy, because I am *bound* to assert my will. All are unhappy because all are afraid and so poor because he has been afraid to assert his will in the highest point and has shown his self-will only in little things, like a schoolboy, I am awfully unhappy, for I'm awfully afraid. Terror is the curse of man. But I will assert my will, I am bound to believe I don't believe. I will begin and will make an end of it and open the door, and will save. That's the only thing that will save mankind and will re-create the next generation physically; for with his present physical nature man can't get on without his former God, I believe. For three years I've been seeking for the attribute of my godhead and I've found it; the attribute of my godhead is self-will! That's all I can do to prove in the highest point my independence and my new terrible freedom. For it is very terrible. I am killing myself to prove my independence and my new terrible freedom.[5]

This was an early and radical statement of existentialism, set against the background of Russian Orthodoxy. Kirillov, *first*, asserts the necessity for the death of God. The assertion of God's non-existence is with Kirillov the required step for the "liberation" of men. But, *second*, if God is dead, then man is god, and all things are then permitted. This, however, is a fearful conclusion for a generation reared to believe in God and to keep God's law. The man taking this step moves into total freedom, "the greatest glory," but, in the process of becoming his own god, this man carries with him the baggage of the old

---

5. Fyodor Dostoyevsky, *The Possessed* (New York, N.Y.: Modern Library, 1936 edition), 629f.

God. He is full of fear and terror, of self-condemnation, because he is haunted by the moral law of the old God. By killing himself, the leader, Kirillov, places himself beyond the rule or law of the old God. *Third*, to be one's own god is a fearful burden for Kirillov, because one is then *bound* to assert his self-will. The Christian God gave a peace and security by barring certain acts of man's will as evil. But, as one's own god, when man sees something he desires, why should he not take it? Why should he not kill, steal, rape, and lie at will? Restraint is then a self-denial of one's divinity. *Fourth*, the attribute of man's new-found godhead is *self-will*. How can one be a god and deny that? Kirillov committed suicide as a pilot to mankind, to tell them to despise life itself, if it keeps them in bondage to the old God and His law.

But Kirillov came out of the context of a church-oriented culture. While he denied the being of God, he in practice affirmed it. Pyotr Stepanovich, while wrongly stating that Kirillov would not commit suicide, rightly observed, "The nuisance of it is that he believes in God like any priest."[6] The true unbelievers were living beyond God; they were the possessed, the true devils, because for them the only course in their Godless world was the evil act. They practiced evil as a witness to their freedom and the non-being of God and man.

Evil is today endemic in the modern world. The young commit meaningless acts of violence and murder simply to act, to express themselves, and living for them means doing evil. Their self-definition is not in terms of any traditional doctrine of evil: it is in terms of evil, of killing, fornicating mindlessly, and in contempt for all that is good.

I once visited a university student in prison. He simply assumed the meaninglessness of life and being, and Darwin was his one authority. Having a deep respect for his grandmother, it took me years to speak openly of that brilliant young man's views. For him, *to be* meant to commit evil; the ideas of the good, the true, and the holy were myths to him. Man could

---

6. *Ibid.*, 633.

only know himself in what the Church has called evil. Nothing in life had for him any reality other than self-will and evil. If any *being* of a transcendental source existed, it had to be from below, mindless, self-assertive, and essentially chaos. This young man expressed the faith which increasingly manifests itself around the world.

Chapter 15

Truth

Truth is a subject of less and less concern to modern man. *The Dictionary of the History of Ideas* (1974) carries no separate entry on "Truth," although the Index volume has a number of references to it. D.D. Resnes' *Dictionary of Philosophy* (1960) carried entries on "Truth" and five related concepts (Truth, semantical; Truth-function; etc.). Charles A. Baylis, in his entry on "Truth," distinguished between three concepts concerning the nature of truth. *First*, the Correspondence Theory holds that a proposition or meaning is true if there is a corresponding fact. If we say, "It is raining here now," this is true if it is indeed raining here now. *Second*, the Coherence Theory holds that a proposition is true "insofar as it is a necessary constituent of a systematically coherent whole." The absolute, as the one systematic coherent whole, best fits this requirement. *Third*, the Pragmatic Concept is that a proposition is true insofar as it works.[1]

This is, on the whole, an adequate statement. Variations can be fitted into this framework. On the whole, however, this is an intellectual and rationalistic framework. In John 14:6, we

[1]. Charles A. Baylis, "Truth," in Dagobert D. Runes, editor, *Dictionary of Philosophy* (New York, N.Y.: Philosophical Library, 1960), 321f.

are told, "Jesus saith unto him, I am the way, the truth, and the life: no man cometh unto the Father but by me." It is possible to place this statement under Baylis' second concept, but only at the cost of rendering meaningless Jesus' statement. John 1:17 declares, "For the law was given by Moses, but grace and truth came by Jesus Christ." Truth came into this world as a person; this is a statement which shatters Baylis' framework.

But Baylis' statement is still important because it describes how non-Christian men have thoughts. More exactly, for most people until recently the correspondence and the coherence theories have prevailed. Truth is what the facts are, or, truth is whatever is a part of a consistent and coherent whole.

Modern philosophy has increasingly held to the pragmatic view of truth, although under a variety of names. Friedrich Nietzsche, in *Beyond Good and Evil*, affirmed the pragmatic view, so that a lie, being more useful, can be better than the truth. He held that a lie is a condition of life; truth confers no advantage and often means a serious disadvantage.

Nietzsche, however, wrote when the issue of truth versus falsehood was still an important one to the community of intellectuals and educators. Since then, pragmatism has won too thorough a victory, and the issue is held to be a dead one as to whether or not truth is important. In a famous lawsuit of the 1980s and 1990s, the issue was whether or not an interviewer had the right to invent statements and attribute them to the man interviewed. In the 1990s, cases have occurred where statements, incidents, and sequences have been invented and presented as history. To question such falsehoods is regarded as naïve. There are those who regard a concern for truth as a relic of Christianity unfit for a post-Christian era.

At the same time, truth is less relevant in courts of law, where perjury is commonplace and its punishment is rare. Some feel that it is naïve to expect witnesses to tell the truth: that is for the jury to sift out. Paradoxically, even as lying goes unpunished when done under oath, we have the development of a strange doctrine called "truth in advertising." The

Associated Advertising Clubs of the World, in a conference in America in 1911, first formulated the idea of "Truth in Advertising." It was in time used against the advertisers. It was never intended to mean as in court "the truth, the whole truth, and nothing but the truth." The courts in Britain (1891) and the U.S. began to insist that advertising is a promise, and non-delivery an offense. Hyperbole and what was once called "a reasonable flourish" were banned, i.e., slogans like "Worth a guinea a box," or "Pure as the tear that falls upon a sister's grave" (a port wine slogan). The result has been a struggle between the advertiser and the consumer. How to suggest something without incurring a liability?[2] At the same time, the courts seem to believe that the advertisement must be incapable of giving any misconception to the simplest idiot.

Thus, at the same time that courts of law have grown indulgent of perjury, an extreme standard of truth has been established for advertisers. This has been due more to an anti-capitalist mentality than to any concern for truth. This represents, therefore, not a concern for the truth but an animosity to a particular segment of society.

In some sense, it is still a testimony to an older doctrine of truth, in that it recognizes that many people have a lingering loyalty to that ancient doctrine. In civil government, for example, congressional investigations use this old loyalty to the truth to impugn various persons and groups. The idea of a real truth is used pragmatically.

There is another aspect to this question. The non-pragmatic doctrines of truth, whether Christian or non-Christian, relate to some doctrine of God, or the Absolute, something transcendent. But what if *truth* is related to something else? The new doctrine of the ultimate will alter radically one's concept of *truth*. The great change brought in by the Enlightenment, and made emotionally central by man like Rousseau, was Nature. The Marquis de Sade made the

---

2. "Truth in Advertising," in Geoffrey Grigson and Charles Harvard Gibbs-Smith, editors, *Ideas* (New York, N.Y.: Hawthorne Books, 1957), 403f.

substitution and developed it systematically. If the God of Scripture is the Supreme Being, then His law-revelation and His incarnation in Christ define the truth. However, if Nature is ultimate, then the truth is whatever occurs in Nature, and the lie is whatever opposes Nature, i.e., Biblical law and morality. The truth meant for Sade and his successors murder, rape, incest, sodomy, etc. Nothing in Nature requires the punishment of any such acts.[3] The result is a moral revolution: God and His Son are evil, and Satan is good and the champion of freedom. To revolt against God is to revolt against oppression and tyranny, in this perspective. The whole moral world is turned upside down.

Thus, while in part the ancient doctrines of good and evil survive as the belief of many, in practice a new concept has replaced them. If man is ultimate, as he is to the humanistic and existentialist perspective, the truth is what man, the new god, declares it is. There can be no higher frame of reference than man in such thinking.

But man in the modern worldview represents a strange contradiction. He is, *first*, the highest point of evolution, a self-conscious being who is both a definer and a creator. But, *second*, he is a part of an evolutionary process and a passive product who is only marginally self-conscious. Most of his life lies in his unconscious being. This means that he can be manipulated, and should be. This is a doctrine which invites totalitarianism.[4] This means commonly "power for its own sake," and the "enjoyment also in the power to humiliate."[5] Powdermaker, writing of this with respect to Hollywood and the film industry, concluded:

> Hollywood had the elaborated totalitarian elements we have described: the concept of people as property and as objects to be manipulated, highly concentrated and

3. Donald Thomas, *The Marquis de Sade* (New York, N.Y.: Citadel Press, 1992), 172.
4. Hortense Powdermaker, *Hollywood, The Dream Factory* (Boston, Massachusetts: Little, Brown, 1950), 327.
5. *Ibid.*, 329.

> personalized power for power's sake, an amorality, and an atmosphere of breaks, continuous anxiety and crisis.[6]

I have at various times written and spoken about modern man's will to fiction. Never before in history has man's time been more devoted to the unreal, to fiction. He feeds on this in films, novels, television, and in other ways. A considerable amount of his time goes into a passive submission to such fiction because modern man wants it. The Twentieth Century has been dominated by this will to fiction. Much of its politics has been marked by its intensely cultivated love of fiction. This should surprise no one. When people turn their backs on God's truth, they will hunger for untruth, for fiction, and they will *live* in the world of their imagination. It is always surprising how much people are given over in their imagination to hopelessly unrealistic ideas and emotions. Such imaginings are a product of modern humanistic education. People are encouraged to hope for and dream about things impossible for them. To cite a very obvious example, a widow in her fifties found films, television, and popular music as marvelous stimuli to encourage her to think of herself in romantic terms about a young man in his twenties. An attempt to help her to think realistically and practically was described as hateful and mean.

In all such thinking, *truth* is a totally subjective concept; it is equated with what the person feels and wants.

A world with no more truth than this is not only living a lie, but is also committing suicide.

---

6. *Ibid.*, 332.

Chapter 16

Accidental Man

A change of culture means a change of language. The languages of Christendom have been more shaped by the Bible than people realize. Language reveals how we think, or do not think. One can see, in the dramatic changes in the language of youth from 1900 to the 1990s, how the faith and culture of the United States has been altered.

Western languages, well into the Twentieth Century, reflected also the Greco-Roman heritage. The vocabulary of thought was often classical, or an attempted fusion of the Christian and the classical. In fact, there is a philosophy of language, and the discipline has a variety of emphases. What is language in essence, and what does grammar tell us about thinking? These and like questions are not our concern here, other than to point out the complexity of the subject.

A related subject is vocabulary. Our vocabulary reveals the perimeters, the boundaries, of our mind and of our thinking. Man has always been speaking-man, from Eden to the present never the primitive grunter of evolutionary fiction. However much some youth today seem to be imitating the fictional grunters, they remain human beings, persons, albeit sinful ones.

The old vocabulary of Christendom spoke of *substance* and *accident. Substance* (Latin *sub* plus *stare*, and the Greek *hypo* plus *stasis*, to stand under) refers to the basic reality in, under, or behind things. The *accident* of things is that which changes, is on the surface. It is related to our idea of the *accidental.* The word comes from the Latin *accidens*, *acciders*, to happen, chance, a befalling, any fortuitous or non-essential property. The idea of *chance* was important in Greek thought; in Christian thought the word *accident* came to mean non-essential. Aquinas summarized it clearly in two statements: "That which is outside the substance of a thing, and yet is belonging to the thing, is called an accident of it." Again, an accident is "That whose nature is to exist in another."

The language of substance and accident was very important to Western thought until the rise of Darwinism. What Darwin insisted on was the sole "reality," and the triumph of chance. All things developed out of nothing through chance. The only "reality" is chance: there is no "substance" to the universe or multiverse, only "accidents," chance.

But with Darwin *substance* was leached out of the universe and replaced with the omnipresence of chance. It was at this point that much criticism was leveled against Darwin. The world was ready to accept evolution as against God, but Darwin's theory, despite a slight blow to "design," actually stressed chance variations. Thomas Huxley tried to defend Darwin at this point, declaring,

> But probably the best answer to those who talk of Darwinism meaning the reign of "chance," is to ask them what they themselves understand by "chance?" Do they believe that anything in this universe happens without reason or without cause? Do they really conceive that any event has no cause, and could not have been predicted by any one who had a sufficient insight into the order or Nature? If they do, it is they who are the inheritors of antique superstition and ignorance, and whose minds have never been illumined by a ray of scientific thought. The one act of faith in the convert to science, is validity in all times and under all circumstances, of the law of causation.

> This confession is an act of faith, because by the nature of the case, the truth of such propositions is not susceptible of proof. But such faith is not blind, but reasonable; because it is invariably confirmed by experience, and constitutes the sole trustworthy foundation for all action.[1]

Huxley knew better. He used a strategy commonplace to scientists since then of accusing critics of superstition and ignorance. With great condescension, the critic is treated as a man too ignorant to know what he is criticizing and as one who is painfully uncomprehending. The plain fact was that chance is basic to Darwin's perspective and to evolution.

It still is. Hudson Hoagland, then Executive Director of the Worcester Foundation for Experimental Biology, wrote that there are "only two answers to the question of how life began. It must either have risen spontaneously from nonliving material or have been created by supernatural means." For Hoagland, the second alternative means "science has nothing to contribute, since the question cannot be resolved by the operational approaches of science."[2] For Hoagland, chance can explain everything.[3] For him, "Evolution is creative, but its creativity is independent of purpose or design."[4]

R.W. Gerard, M.D., then of the University of Michigan, held that man's morals are *accidents* of his time and place.[5] This is a logical conclusion. The universe and all things within it have been stripped of substance. The existence of God is more than denied: it is dismissed as an unscientific and irrelevant question. Is it any wonder that all that remains of man is *accidental m*an? He is not a being created in the image of God (Gen. 1:21-28). Rather, he is a struggling product of evolution, lacking in definition by substance. He is a product of chance.

---

1. Thomas Huxley, "On the Reception of the 'Origin of Species,'" in Francis Darwin, editor, *The Life and Letters of Charles Darwin*, vol. 1 (New York, N.Y.: Basic Books, 1959), 553.
2. Hudson Hoagland, "The Elements of Life," in Lyman Bryson, editor, *An Outline of Man's Knowledge of the Modern World* (Garden City, New York: Nelson Doubleday, 1960), 152.
3. *Ibid.*, 152f.
4. *Ibid.*, 159.
5. *Ibid.*, 73-89.

Emile Durkheim (1858-1917), in his *Rules of Sociological Method* (1894), viewed criminals as evolutionary pioneers, exploring by their activities the next step in the evolution of man. Man for Durkheim had no fixed nature nor morality. He was an accident of an evolutionary process, and his accidental nature would change and develop with time. For those in this tradition, the criminal is an interesting figure and an important one. It was altogether logical for Jean-Paul Sartre to take a homosexual criminal and hail him as Saint Genet, Actor and Martyr (1963). Precisely because for Sartre and Genet God was denied, the new idea of the sacred was transferred to evil. The dedication to pure evil made Genet sacred in Sartre's eyes.[6] God having been denied, there is no longer any true substance in all the universe. The accidental man, by his total dedication to an anti-God faith, affirms thereby the validity of the *accident* only, and the accident without *substance* has no point of reference and no meaning. Time in this framework has no meaning. "Sacred time is cyclical: it is the time of Eternal Recurrence."[7] The sacred has thus become the meaningless, the evil, not the good. This is the triumph of the *accident*, and hence of accidental man.

Let us consider the meaning of this *pure* evil, this triumph of the *accident* over *substance.* One of the characteristics of life in the Western world since, at least, 1960 has been the rise of mindless crime. Drive-by shootings, the random killing of innocent people, and the ready indulgence and torture of people who have done nothing are examples of mindless crimes, uncaused evil. Now Christian ethics has sought to further good for good's sake, not a self-serving virtue but one motivated by gratitude toward God for His goodness. Rather than a man-centered cause for self-promotion, Christian virtue is required to be goodness for goodness sake, virtue for virtue's sake. The Christian must not avoid murder, adultery, or theft out of fear of the consequence, but out of a love of God and His moral law, out of a love for virtue. Virginity and chastity

---

6. *Ibid.*, 215f., 261.
7. *Ibid.*,13.

are not to be adhered to out of a desire to gain a better spouse, a better reputation, or to avoid disease, but out of a regard for virginity and chastity as the true way of life, for virtue's sake.

Now evil seeks the same purity of dedication to evil. The purely professional criminal is in crime for the money, for profit. He has no desire to do more than steal or kill as necessary. The perpetrators of mindless crime may steal or kill, but their basic objective is evil. A young man who enjoyed seducing and then leaving girls who were virgins responded, when someone asked him why he went after some girls who had no special appeal. His response was, he wanted them because they were virgins. The appeal was evil for evil's sake; it was despoiling virtue. The accidental man hates the substantive life, and he wants to prove that it is a fraud by destroying it.

In an interview with Fareed Zakaria, managing editor of *Foreign Affairs*, Lee Kuan Yew, prime minister of Singapore, except for an interlude, from 1959-1990, when he allowed his deputy to succeed him, spoke of the change in the United States (and elsewhere) that had lessened his admiration and respect. "Westerners have abandoned an ethical basis for society, believing that all problems are solvable by a good government, which we in the East never believed possible."[8]

Centuries ago, the East was wealthy and powerful, but certain ideas it held had evil consequences. Buddha's belief in ultimate nothingness was destructive of cultural strength and morality. In China, philosophy preceded Hume by many centuries in its epistemological skepticism. One philosopher questioned the real world; he held that it was difficult to say whether or not the "dream" world or the "waking" world was real. Such thinking meant cultural paralysis because in its own way it reduced humanity to the level of the accidental man.

As reported by the Lofton Letter,

---

8. Fareed Zakaria, "Culture is Destiny," in *Foreign Affairs*, March-April, 1994, 112.

> According to the George Barna Research Group, four out of 10 people who call themselves evangelicals don't believe there is such a thing as absolute truth. Says Barna, "It's pretty frightening." Of all U.S. adults, 71 percent reject the idea of absolute truth.[9]

To reject absolute Truth is to reject Christianity. The only God possible in such a universe, and the only logical Christ, comes out of the cosmic accident. God and Christ then, if existing, are simply struggling in a cosmic accident to gain some kind of relevance. There can then be no absolute God, no decree of predestination, and no substance to law and morality, nor to man. Because the Western world has become the realm of accidental man, it is in danger of becoming the realm of fading men and fading cultures and nations.

Accidental man is oblivious to all this. He believes God to be dead, and, because of this absurdity, is himself dying.

---

9. *Lofton Letter*, 19; March, 1994.

Chapter 17

"Integration into the Void"

In his study of the *Psychology of Religion* (1935), Dr. Cornelius Van Til called attention to the difference between the Christian and the modern view of man and his psychology:

> ...The activity by which personality realizes itself to be sure, very genuine and significant but it is genuine and significant only because it acts before the background of the plan of God. The integration of personality, that is, the constant readjustment of the particular and the universal within itself, and the constant readjustment of the whole personality as an individual to the universal found in the universe beyond itself, takes place by a more ultimate and constant readjustment of the individual together with his surroundings to God who is the absolute particular and the absolute universal combined in one ultimate personality. The integration of personality, according to the Christian view, is an integration toward and by virtue of an ultimate self-sufficient personality.
>
> In contrast with this the modern concept of the integration of personality is an integration into the void. We can best appreciate this if we note that *the concept purpose itself has been completely internalized.*[1]

[1] Cornelius Van Til, *Psychology of Religion* (Philadelphia, Pennsylvania: Westminster Seminary, 1935), 59f.

The emphasis in humanistic, evolutionary psychology is not on knowing man in terms of the image of God in him, but on looking backward on the evolutionary ladder. The child is thus the key to the adult: primitive man determines modern man, and primordial man is to be understood in terms of his animal inheritance. We have an integration downward into the void.

Various modern psychologies have differing views of man, but they agree on man's evolutionary and primitive past as the key to his present. Thus Sigmund Freud found his explanation in the belief (as set forth by Robertson Smith) that man's basic nature, as determined by his primordial ancestors, is the will to kill the father, to copulate with the mother and sisters, and to eat the father.

But God created the first man as a full-grown man. His problem is not a primitive origin, but sin. He is responsible to God, but the human being of evolution is responsible to nothing and to no one. In Van Til's words,

> The real reason why modern psychology has left no room or responsibility is found in the fact that it has taken the whole of the human personality in all its aspects, self-conscious and sub-conscious, and immersed it in an ultimate metaphysical void. Man cannot be responsible to the void. Hence the only way in which man can establish human responsibility is by showing the ultimate irrationalism of all non-theistic thought of which modern psychology is but a particular manifestation. In that way we place man self-consciously and sub-consciously in every aspect of his person before the personality of God. Man is responsible in the whole of his personality but only if he is the creature of God. Man *before God* is the only alternative to man *in the world*.[2]

Modern irresponsible and lawless man is the inevitable product of modern evolutionary thought. If man is to be explained in terms of an animal past, then man, with more intelligence, will far exceed animals in his rapacity because he believes he knows that there is nothing that can restrain him. Humanistic

2. *Ibid.*, 62.

religions, Van Til added, become means of adjustment and integration into the void.[3]

Because of man's Cainitic wish that there be no God, he prefers the void to God and God's holy purpose. He dedicates himself to the destruction of all meaning from above. Reverence for Nature replaces reverence for God. One result has been Gaia worship, the uncritical worship of the natural world.

To cite one example, Alan S. Miller, retired Academic Coordinator and Senior Lecturer in the Department of Conservation and Resource Studies, the University of California at Berkeley, is the author of the book, *Gaia, Connections: An Introduction to Ecology, Ecoethics and Economics.* For him, "ecological health is an uniquely feminist issue." As a result, he sees as "a minimal set of affirmations" the following:

> 1. There are important and necessary connections between the oppression and exploitation of women and the oppression and exploitation of nature,
>
> 2. An understanding and comprehension of the nature of these connections is very much necessary to any adequate understanding of the double oppression around us of women and of nature.
>
> 3. All feminist theory and practice must therefore include an ecological perspective to be whole.
>
> 4. Any solution to ecological problems it follows, must include a feminist perspective in order to comprehend the problem.[4]

Smith's position is more logical than that of many who disagree with him. The further from Nature, the less ethical man becomes, so that a patriarchal class is seen as an oppressing class. Smith bases ethics on "the entire world of nature" rather than "simply on human beings."[5]

---

3. *Ibid.*, 134.
4. Alan S. Miller, "Gaia Connections," in *The Mountain Chronicles Harbinger*, vol. 2, no. 4; Spring, 1994, 18. Arnold, California; *paraphrased.*
5. *Ibid.*, 18, 34.

Implicit in Gaia worship is the belief that women are more primitive and natural and therefore closer to Nature than men, especially patriarchal Christian men. The ethics of Gaia worship are usually anti-Christian and affirmative of moral practices forbidden in God's law.

This integration downward into the void has not been restricted to feminism and environmentalism. Modern art was a leader in this effort. It was marked early in the Twentieth Century to a hostility to order and to form. It deconstructed both man and nature, and it approved of a disintegration of norms.

Telling indictments of modern art have been written in great numbers, as, for example, William Snaith's *The Irresponsible Arts* (1964). Their weakness is that they bypass the revolt against God which is a revolt against purpose, patterns, and meaning in every sphere. Alan Levy wrote about *The Culture Vultures* (1968); but, in a world without God, what is wrong with vultures? They are an aspect of nature.

The student revolution of the 1960s has been accurately described by Peter Collier and David Horowitz in *The Destructive Generation* (1989). Many of the students were not only destructive but childish; they took a delight in urinating and defecating publicly, using obscene language, and copulating on campus-grounds. This was an aspect of their integration downward into the void. Having rejected authority from above, that of God, parents, community, police, university officials, and others, they affirmed in practice an affirmation of "things below." The criminal became even a folk hero to some.

The willful blindness to anything but power from below marked more than students. Paul Davies and John Gribbin, in *The Matter Myth* (1992), give an excellent account of the death of the long established premises of materialism. They write at times as though the only logical alternative to the old science is creationism, but they specifically reject it. They recognize that "All science is founded on the assumption that the physical world is ordered." Physics is the most powerful expression of this order. "Nobody knows where these laws come from nor why they operate universally and unfailingly."[6] In spite of this, Davies and Gribbin insist of "seeing" that the Earth may be "in some sense, ...a simple living organism," Gaia.[7] The word *atom* may be no more than a code word rather than "an independent part of reality," but Gaia is more real than the atom.[8] The authors even raise, in passing, a question about heliocentricity (19f), but they do not consider God and creationism as an option; their source is the void.

An environmentalist has observed that, as he looks at nature and what man has done to it, he is ashamed of being a man. This is a new definition of sin, and a logical one. Sin is any offense against whatever is ultimate in our universe of thought. If God is ultimate, then sin is any want of conformity to the law of God (1 John 3:4). If Nature is ultimate, then sin is any violation of that world of Nature. For Albert Schweitzer, this meant that he did not kill insects, and he picked up worms, after a rain, to replace them on the earth, lest they be stepped on in the pathways. It also troubled his conscience to be killing germs as a doctor. With his "reverence for life," sin was an offense against worms, insects, any and every form of life.

Every religion has its own concept of ultimacy, and it defines sin in terms of it. The growing Sadean faith of our time goes beyond such Eastern cults as the Jains to assert a most radical contempt of man in the name of worshipping Nature. The record of paganism is not a good one. Hinduism's reverence for animal life has gone hand-in-hand with the caste system, indifference to suffering, and mass killings, such as the many millions killed when India gained "freedom" after World War II. The rise of the Sadean faith in the West has been accompanied by the phenomenal increase in all kinds of crimes. Crimes of violence against people can *perhaps* be

---

6. Paul Davies and John Gribbin, *The Matter Myth* (New York, N.Y.: Simon & Shuster, 1992), 30.
7. *Ibid.*, 285, 287f.
8. *Ibid.*, 28, cf., 27, 35f.

explained by the hatred of many against mankind as the ostensibly evil animal, raping the earth. Then why do so many set fires to forests? Is not Gaia worship to some degree not only a hatred of man, but also of life?

Evolution was once seen as identical with progress, so that man was the high point of all being. That faith in an inevitable progress is now waning, if not gone. Sade rejected God and therefore life. His demand was for a universal death, and the same death wish is present in his heirs and followers. Proverbs 8:35-36 tells us,

> 35. For whoso findeth me findeth life, and shall obtain favour of the LORD.
> 36. But he that sinneth against me wrongeth his own soul: all they that hate me love death.

Chapter 18

Power

Original sin, according to Genesis 3:5, is man's desire to be his own god, knowing or determining good and evil for himself, becoming his own source for all law and morality. Man seeks to be his own god in *rebellion against God.* Man's will to be god does not mean emulating the goodness, grace, or mercy of God. Albert Camus stated the goal clearly: "Since God claims all that is good in man, it is necessary to decide what is good and choose what is evil."[1] The focus is on power, man's desire to play god by the exercise, if possible, of total power. Horrifying stories are told of the vicious delight of the Bolsheviks in their treatment of the men and women of the old order.

This was nothing new in history. The terrorism used by ancient Assyria, the destruction of life, property, and marriage by the Mazdakites of Persia in the fifth century A.D., the French and Russian Revolutions, and, indeed, the routine conduct of warfare over the centuries is a long tale of wilful atrocities. For example, Ghingis Khan held,

1. Albert Camus, *The Rebel* (New York, N.Y.: Vintage Books, 1956), 21.

> The greatest pleasure is to vanquish your enemies and chase them before you, to rob them of their wealth and see those dear to them bathed in tears, to ride their horses and clasp to your bosom their wives and daughters.[2]

This language is close to that of modern de-Christianized men when liquor loosens their tongues.

But this lust for power takes forms other than that of Ghingis Khan's. It can be scientific; it can be expressed in the desire to control or to create life. Gena Corea, a feminist, has written *The Mother Machine, Reproductive Technologies from Artificial Insemination to Artificial Wombs* (1985), a horrifying account of the experimentations with birth. The results are commonly deadly, but the experiments continue. The dream is, among other things, to produce babies through men made into artificial females. Some have claimed to have transplanted mouse embryos into male mice.[3] The desire for the power to control is so great that physicians in one medical journal actually wrote,

> It may well be that during the next 42 years the allowing of a vaginal delivery or attempted vaginal delivery may need to be justified in each particular instance. Perhaps it is not altogether too provocative to suggest that vaginal delivery may yet become the exception rather than the rule.[4]

Eggs are apparently taken from women without their consent, to be used in experimentation.[5]

Too commonly, those in power equate intelligence with power, so that they see other people as experimental animals, and themselves as working for science and therefore justified in their planning. Dostoyevsky's Grand Inquisitor (in *The Brothers Karamazov*) equated his controls with wisdom and the

---

2. James Chambers, *The Devil's Horsemen, The Mongol Invasion of Europe* (New York, N.Y.: Atheneum, 1979), 6.
3. Gena Corea, *The Mother Machine, Reproductive Technologies from Artificial Insemination to Artificial Wombs* (New York, N.Y.: Harper & Row, 1985), 291f.
4. *Ibid.*, 97.
5. *Ibid.*, 101.

good of mankind. He saw Christ's position as unrealistic because it required freedom, personal decision and conversion. The Grand Inquisitor tells Christ,

> Oh, ages are yet to come of the confusion of free thought, of their science and cannibalism. For having begun to build their tower of Babel without us, they will end, of course, with cannibalism. But then the beast will crawl to us and lick our feet and spatter them with tears of blood. And we shall sit upon the beast and raise the cup, and on it will be written, "Mystery." But then, and only then, the reign of peace and happiness will come for men. Thou art proud of Thine elect, but Thou hast only the elect, while we give rest to all. And besides, how many of those elect, those mighty ones who could become elect, have grown weary waiting for Thee, and have transferred and will transfer the powers of their spirit and the warmth of their heart to the other camp, and end by raising their *free* banner against Thee. Thou didst Thyself lift up that banner. But with us all will be happy and will no more rebel nor destroy one another as under Thy freedom. Oh, we shall persuade them that they will only become free when they renounce their freedom to us and submit to us.
>
> And shall we be right or shall we be lying? They will be convinced that we are right, for they will remember the horrors of slavery and confusion to which Thy freedom brought them. Freedom, free thought and science, will lead them unto such straits and will bring them face to face with such marvels and insoluble mysteries, that some of them, the fierce and rebellious, will destroy themselves, others, rebellious will destroy themselves, others, rebellious but weak, will destroy one another, while the rest, weak and unhappy, will crawl fawning to our feet and whine to us: "Yes, you were right, you alone possess His mystery, and we come back to you, save us from ourselves."[6]

Dostoyevsky's Grand Inquisitor contrasts the freedom of the Spirit against a controlling Church which distrusts freedom. Dostoyevsky saw things as still in the framework of

---

6. Fyodor Dostoyevsky, *The Brothers Karamazov*. Constance Garnett translation. (New York, N.Y.: The Modern Library, 1937 edition), 267f.

Christendom, whereas George Orwell, in *1984* (1948), viewed the scene in terms of the growing power of humanistic socialism. For Orwell's new men, God is dead; He is also forgotten. Truth and meaning are man-made, not God-given. One of the three main Party slogans in Oceania is "FREEDOM IS SLAVERY." A second is, "BIG BROTHER IS WATCHING YOU," and the third, "WAR IS PEACE." These and their implementations serve to obliterate man as God created him in order to create the state-made man. One of the tragedies of Orwell's life is that, much as he hated this goal, he believed it to be possible, and, in fact, in process of realization. Aldous Huxley's *Brave New World* had not gone quite so far in its pessimism. Modern man's dreams of utopia have become dystopias. Science fiction writers have transferred the utopian dream to distant planets and galaxies, but they have only succeeded in transplanting original sin and the struggle for power across the cosmos. Feminism has extended the power struggle into the relationship of the sexes. The children's rights advocates see the power struggle as indigenous to family life.

Having denied God and His law, modern man has denied any morality other than a self-made and purely personal one. The ethics propounded by philosophers, politicians, and educators have no God-given and eternal value. They are pragmatically created and pragmatically abandoned, even as treaties between nations are.

Charles Oliver, the astute commentator for *Reason*, has cited a telling incident,

> Andy Hansen's parents weren't too pleased when he brought home a C in math, so they did the only thing good parents can do: They sued his teacher. After a year and $4,000 in legal fees ($8,500 for the Contra Costa County, California, school district), the Hansens got a verdict: The C stands. The father says he'll appeal. "We went in and tried to make a deal. They wanted a C, we wanted an A,

> so why not compromise on a B. But they dug in their heels, and here we are."[7]

If the child only earned a C, why not a C? No ethical consideration is cited, only the desire to have one's will done. This is the modern mood. Self-will and power govern modern man.

James W. McGray has summarized the difference between Dostoyevsky's Grand Inquisitor and Orwell's O'Brien very aptly: "For the Inquisitors of old, God is love. But, for the new Inquisitors, God is Pure Power."[8]

Orwell's vision of this new order stresses power: the future is a boot stamping on a human face forever. This is the logical conclusion of Genesis 3:5, of the tempter's program. It is a vision of death.

---

7. Charles Oliver, "Brickbats," in *Reason*, April, 1994, 15.
8. James W. McGray, "The Golden Rule and Paternalism," in *Journal of Interdisciplinary Studies*, vol. 1, no. 1, 2, 1989.

Chapter 19

Revolution and Death

There are two remarkable passages in Job that tell us much about Satan. The first, Job 1:9-11, has a startling nature: Satan expresses a *total* distrust in any goodness in man:

> 9. Then Satan answered the LORD and saith, Doth Job fear God for nought?
> 10. Hast not thou made an hedge about him, and about his house, and about all that he hath on every side? thou hast blessed the work of his hands, and his substance is increased in the land.
> 11. But put forth thine hand now, and touch all that he hath, and he will curse thee to thy face.

Again, after Job is sore smitten, Satan demands more testing, saying,

> 4. And Satan answered the LORD, and said, Skin for skin, yea, all that a man hath will be give for his life.
> 5. But put forth thine hand now, and touch his bone and his flesh, and he will curse thee to thy face (Job 2:4-5).

Satan sees man as totally, irreparably depraved. For him, the creature can only be governed by self-interest, and Satan sees God as naïve and ignorant because of His confidence in Job. Satan's cynicism is an exercise in self-justification. Being himself fallen, and because his will is to be his own god, he sees all mankind as incapable of any other course than self-will. His temptation in the Garden of Eden was to declare that every man can be his own god, determining good and evil for himself (Gen. 3:5). The only "good" will is self-will. There is no absolute and binding-norm or law. Every man lives beyond God's good and evil, and determines his own law and morality. Thus, in terms of God's law, all men are eternally evil. For Satan, liberation comes in living beyond God's law and beyond God's plan for man.

This same perspective governs Satan's temptation of Jesus Christ in the wilderness. In the Greek text, Satan does not say, "If thou be *the* son of God" (Matt. 4:3, 6), but rather, "If thou be *a* son of God." Despite this expressed cynicism, Satan knew whom he had before him. His temptations are important in telling us what his plan and purpose are. The *first* temptation is to minister to mankind's economic needs: turn these stones into bread (Matt. 4:3). If God has the holy and righteous or just character He claims, why does He allow the poor to remain poor and hungry? This is a declaration of the priority of need over faith, of welfarism over character. *Second*, Satan demands that Jesus Christ make faith unnecessary by a public demonstration of angelic power and rescue. Why should men be compelled to manifest faith under adversity and fire? *Third*, Satan demands that Christ fall down and worship him as the true friend and liberator of mankind. Satan thereby declares himself to be the true liberation and messiah of mankind. Satan sees himself as the one who delivers man from the bondage of God, law, and morality. Every man can, then, realize his own potential apart from God. Man must think of his own possibilities positively and reject the judgments of God and His law against himself.

By this, Satan has reversed the moral order. He sees God as evil, as hostile to human potentiality. In a sense, God is the *unreal* because His requirements go against the reality of man. For Satan, The Fall and the expulsion from Eden, represent God's evil hostility to man's attempt to liberate himself. For him, the idea of God as the lawgiver and Redeemer is an illegitimate pretension. God *may* be the source of all things, but for Satan this does not make Him the controller, nor lawgiver. Far from it.

St. Paul tells us in 2 Corinthians 11:13-15:

> 13. For such are false apostles, deceitful workers, transforming themselves into the apostles of Christ.
> 14. And no marvel; for Satan himself is transformed into an angel of light.
> 15. Therefore it is no great thing if his ministers also be transformed as the ministers of righteousness; whose end shall be according to their works.

Neither Satan nor his servants see themselves as the agents of sin and darkness, but rather as liberators, as angels of life. They are in the church, and in the world, to enlighten and to deliver people from their "bondage" to God. They see mankind as enslaved by God, and it is their religious purpose to free humanity. They have their own zealous sense of calling to liberate mankind from bondage to a false doctrine of God, and their true, if unavowed, god is Satan. Such men have been Gnostics, heretics, Modernists, antinomians, and more. They have adulterated the Gospel, often in Christ's name. Their goal is man's salvation rather than the glory of God *because man has priority with them.* The God of Scripture redeems men for His Kingdom and His holy and eternal purposes, not to give men peace of mind and a ticket to heaven.

These pretended angels of light reverse God's order. For them, what the Bible calls evil and sin is *reality*. Because their primary focus is man, they see God's law-word as unreal, remote, and non-pertinent. They mine the Bible for "nuggets" that can be used to minister to men's being. Our Lord says, "Seek ye first the kingdom of God, and his righteousness," or, justice, "and all these things shall be added unto you" (Matt. 6:33). But men reject this: not God's Kingdom and justice but their own peace of mind, deliverance from problems, and so on, are wanted. This is not the gospel of Christ, but the pretended ministries of light.

Now, if the Church is so derelict, should we be surprised that the world is as perverse as it is? There is widespread and growing vindication of evil as good, as *the* good. Men preach on the healing potential in adultery, or teach it in counseling. Abortion and homosexuality are legalized and protected, and so on. What was once called evil is now defended as good, because the sole remaining good, now in process of being made fully legitimate, is to affirm man's freedom to do what he pleases. The one condition is that none be harmed, and that limitation is waning.

Increasingly, the idea of any supernatural power, any purpose in life, or any meaning, is regarded as not only untenable, but unfit for any public forum. Thus, Dean Kenyon, a biologist at San Francisco State University, was forbidden to teach that intelligent design is apparent in the universe. His views are not creationism. An authority on chemical evolutionary theory and the study of origins, he began to doubt the validity of his own work. His expression of doubt led to being forbidden to teach on the subject.[1]

The offense of such teaching as Kenyon's is that it opens up the possibility of a transcendental origin, purpose, or meaning. The modern definition of light is that which comes from below.

A reading of Puritan autobiographies or personal accounts of their spiritual pilgrimage is revelatory of a certain fact, one which, from Augustine on through the medieval era, is very prevalent. While unbelief and cynicism were not uncommon in those eras, so too a lively sense of necessary purpose to life was quite commonplace. As a result, spiritual crises resulted in conversion experiences. Now these crises are emphatically not lacking in our time, but there is a difference.

The background has changed, as the intellectual environment then pointed to some kind of cosmic meaning and purpose. Since Darwin, the intellectual context has

---

1. Stephen C. Myer, "Open the Debate on Life's Origins," in *Insight*, February 21, 1994, vol. 10, no. 8, 26ff.

changed radically. Purpose and meaning from above are denied. During the era from 1920-1940, many books by scientists pointed to a non-Christian purpose in the universe. Such books sold well and were soon forgotten. The academic community treated them with contempt and scorn. However outstanding the qualifications of the scientists, their pursuit of meaning from above rather than below meant their instant disqualification. Their writings were dismissed as regressive, and, in one instance, a professor said of such a scientist that age and the approach of death had led him to wishful thinking. Meaning and purpose were untenable concepts, even though these men believed in evolution, not devolution; if the one be true, why not the other? Chance can work both upward and downward.

This rigid limitation placed on reality is very prevalent in the church world, in seminaries and in colleges. Thus, Father Raymond E. Brown is the recipient of over twenty honorary doctorates from both Catholic and Protestant universities, and professor emeritus of Biblical Studies at Union Theological Seminary, New York, N.Y. He is also the author of *The Birth of the Messiah, A Commentary on the Infancy Narrative in the Gospels of Matthew and Luke* (1977, 1993). The book bears the imprimatur of the Catholic archdiocese of New York. Its emphasis is naturalistic. Father Brown remarks, of the prophecy in Isaiah 7:14 of a virgin birth, that "this conception of prophesy as prediction has disappeared from serious scholarship today."[2] This is a statement of amazing arrogance. "Serious scholarship today" means for Brown scholarship that is *a priori* naturalistic and hostile to the obvious meaning of the Bible. There are more than a few scholars of this century whose view of prophecy is totally different from Brown's. He, however, rejects all contrary opinions as unworthy of consideration. This is the usual modernist dogmatism parading as "objective" and scientific.

---

[2] Raymond E. Brown, *The Birth of the Messiah, A Commentary on the Infancy Narratives in the Gospels of Matthew and Luke* (New York, N.Y.: Doubleday, 1993), 146.

The latter half of the Twentieth Century has not been lacking in intense partisan conflicts, mass protests, demonstrations, and riots, all in the name one cause or another. But this passionate devotion to causes or issues is not matched by a like dedication to religious and moral faith as such. Faith does not command as issues do. Never has hatred been more condemned and more practiced. Kenneth Keniston, in his study of post-World War II youth, saw them as "Strong in opposition…weak in affirmation."[3] Theirs is "the cult of the present." This existential emphasis on the present is existentialist and leads to a radical self-absorption because the governing reality is the self. Together with this there is a greater worth given to protest than to patient, long-term work to reform things. They "prefer 'role-playing' to deep devotion."[4] Keniston observed, with telling clarity,

> A man's sense of his own place in time, and of his place in a society and world located in history, is central to his definition of himself, just as a society's definition of its place in history is one of the most distinguishing features of that society.[5]

But if man has no religious definition of himself in terms of a transcendental order, in terms of the triune God, he will have no meaning that transcends himself. Definition then becomes a problem. What is man? Albert Camus (1913-1960) answered it thus: "I rebel — therefore we exist."[6] Satan, in speaking to Eve, defined himself and mankind by negation, "Yea, hath God said"? (Gen. 3:1).

But whenever man begins to define himself by negation, *against God*, then man's temper becomes revolutionary. He sees himself as chained, and he demands freedom. Revolutionary freedom is the liberty to negate, hate, deface, and kill. Centuries of achievement were destroyed by the

---

3. Kenneth Keniston, *The Uncommitted* (New York, N.Y.: Harcourt, Brace and World, 1960, 1965), 102.

4. *Ibid.*, 236.

5. *Ibid.*, 237.

6. Albert Camus, *The Rebel* (New York, N.Y.: Vintage Books, 1956), 22.

French and Russian Revolutions, for example. The works of great French composers largely disappeared. The great negater, the Marquis de Sade, had his property devastated. The mobs looted his chateau, carried away what they could and smashed what they could not. They did to Sade's chateau what he strove to do to civilization. Beautiful objects were systematically smashed. In the words of Donald Thomas, "Even beauty was now suspect as an emblem of former aristocratic privilege."[7] All this was logical in Sade's world, a universe without God, morality, and law. Revolutionary freedom is the power to destroy and kill without hindrance. The revolutionist seeks to suspend the laws of God and men and to mutilate and smash at will.

Revolution is the basic premise of the modern age because of its anti-Christian character and its determined will to obliterate Christianity and the Christian past. Revolution often comes disguised as education, as in the case of John Dewey (1859-1952). In his lectures, *A Common Faith*, Dewey objected to supernatural Christianity as anti-democratic because it divides men into the saved and the lost, saints and sinners, and in terms of heaven and hell.[8] The immediate application of Dewey's vision was the abolition in some schools of grading, and of passing and failing. But Deweyism does not stop there: it is a totally democratic vision. If no heaven and hell division is tolerable, then no division between the law-abiding citizen and the criminal is tenable. We have seen a major step towards such a democracy in a statement by a prominent U.S. attorney general of the duty of that office to protect the guilty.

When the city of Herculaneum, buried together with Pompeii in the eruption of Vesuvius on A.D. August 24, 79, was excavated an inscription on one wall carried a proverb:

---

7. Donald Thomas, *The Marquis de Sade* (New York, N.Y.: Citadel Press, 1992), 205.

8. John Dewey, *A Common Faith* (New Haven, Conn.: Yale University Press, 1934).

"Who does not know how to defend himself does not know how to survive."[9] The problem now is more serious. A powerful element in the modern world has no intention of defending its civilization because, while murderous towards Christianity, it is suicidal with regard to itself. As Proverbs 8:35-36 tells us,

> 35. For whoso findeth me findeth life, and shall obtain favour of the LORD.
> 36. But he that sinneth against me wrongeth his own soul: all they that hate me love death.

---

9. Joseph D. Deiss, *Herculaneum* (New York, N.Y.: Harper & Row, 1966, 1985), 165.

Chapter 20

Gnosticism

As a university student at Berkeley in the mid-1930s, I was interested in educating myself into the culture of my time. In 1934 and 1935, I had read the translations of classical writers with a growing recognition of their paganism and a sense of shock that these things were regarded as *classics*. I turned, then, to the literature, essays, and histories of the Christian centuries with at times equal dismay. With two writers, I began to explore their sources, William Blake and Herman Melville. This led me to gnosticism and writers as diverse as Jacob Boehme and Emmanuel Swedenborg. Among other things, I picked up a used copy of Swedenborg's *A Dictionary of Correspondences* (1899), compiled from his writings. Without the precision of Swedenborg, all the same, many writers have since his day adopted his gnosticism, and, rather crudely, his concept of correspondences in their fuzzy symbolism. Baudelaire, Victor Hugo, Ralph Waldo Emerson, Karl Marx, Hegel, and others gained much from either Boehme or Swedenborg, or both.

As a result, both at the university and in seminary, I read extensively in gnosticism. The writers of the Christian era have rarely been true gnostics. It has been rather the general theme of gnosticism which has appealed to them.

Christianity, when faithful to Scripture, has stressed God's sovereign grace as the means of our salvation. Not merit but God's grace redeems us and makes us a new creation. What we are in and of ourselves is a fallen human race whose destiny is sin and death. Only in Christ are we a royal race whose purpose is dominion. Apart from Christ, if a man looks into his own being, he finds sin and death.

Gnosticism is elitist. It finds within itself not a fallen man but a spark of deity, an inner light, a contact with the ultimate power. It is closely related to mysticism. However, the god reached through one's own being is amorphous, even unconscious, and a god having within itself both male and female principles. God-knowledge is self-knowledge.

Gnostic thought has both a vagueness as well as a meandering precision. Its world is not the creation of Genesis 1, a clear-cut realm of God-established lines and differences. A variety of emanations and development give to the creation of all things layer upon layer of alien forces, purposes, and goals. Nothing is what it seems to be: all things point to something else and are not comprehensible in terms of themselves. At the same time, lacking the God of Scripture, they lack a common purpose and meaning. *The Nag Hammadi Library in English*, which is edited by J.M. Robinson (1988), gives us clearer texts than do the many fragments previously known, but they still lack a coherency of thought; they are miscellaneous in their ideas because the gnostic world views lack any systematic character. They are given to endless complexities and have a variety of sources: Greek, Chaldean, Jewish, Iranian, and others. While some scholars deny that they are "cloudy" writings, only experts long familiar with the documents can find either a semblance of coherency and beauty in them.

We can best understand the problem of Gnostic texts by looking briefly at predestination. In seminary, I heard a theological professor refer to Calvinism as the triumph of logic over common sense. By common sense he meant whatever agreed with his thinking. He was, however, correct in recognizing Calvinism as the coherent and logical statement of Biblical faith. If God is what He says He is, "I am the LORD, and there is none else" (Isa. 45:6, 14, 21-22, etc.), He is the only ultimate cause, power, and determiner in all creation. There is then, an inner and outer coherency to all things visible and invisible, and the only kind of theology possible is *systemic* theology. Apart from such a theology, systematics wanes and then disappears.

Gnostic thought is anti-systemic. Each school bears the marks of an independent school of thought, borrowing some things, but essentially creative in its approach to the world, to the past, present, and future. The gnostic, or those influenced by gnoticism, gives us a new cosmology and a new history. Although Karl Barth's efforts were to create a new version of orthodoxy, in reality he created a "system" closer to gnosticism than the Reformed Faith. He converted the Bible and Biblical history into a Gnostic myth and then took the older Gnostic myth for modern reality. Biblical. History was, for him not actual nor historical, but "holy history," a gnostic mythology. Those who believed that in the Bible they had God's very word were despised by Barth as the supposedly "blessed professors."[1] Barth and Brunner re-interpreted Christianity with categories as alien as those of the ancient gnostics. In Van Til's words,

> As the chief interpretive category of dialecticism, the Individual takes the place of the ontological trinity in orthodox theology; in it being is exhausted in relation and relation is exclusively internal.[2]

The academic scholar may feel that the identification of Barth, as, in some sense, gnostic is unwarranted. However, one of the key marks of the gnostic is to replace history with myth and to posit a new reality, and this is basic to Barthianism. This is why

1. Cornelius Van Til, *The New Modernism* (Philadelphia, Pennsylvania: Presbyterian and Reformed Publishing Company, 1946), 1.
2. *Ibid.*, 275.

Van Til described it as "the *new* modernism." The Barthians rejected the attempt of the older modernists to find "the historical Jesus," i.e., a "real Jesus" stripped of all supernaturalism. Barth wanted no part of that historical quest any more than did the ancient gnostics.

As we have seen, a characteristic aspect of gnosticism is its anti-historical thrust, or, better, its effort to create a new history. Whether in its Valentinean, Sethian, Basilidian, or other forms, it either rejects history or offers a secret doctrine about the supposedly "real" meaning of Biblical history. In the course of this, the power of the Biblical God is diluted or denied in favor of a multi-causal approach to history. Determination is shifted from God downward.

Another aspect of gnosticism is its common insistence on the presence of male and female elements in the gnostic godhead. This has meant an interest in androgyny, and we may even call androgyny a gnostic belief.[3] Anti-Christianity regularly found interesting the obliteration of sexual differences and indulged in transvestite and other activities with pleasure.[4] An androgynous perspective is commonly congenial to homosexuality, as indeed modern forms of gnosticism seem to be. Certainly, women "prophets" were prominent in early gnostic groups, and feminism has gnostic roots. The early feminists insisted on a female aspect in the godhead, whereas by the 1990s, this was replaced by the worship of mother earth, the goddess Gaia.

Biblical, theological doctrine was replaced by many early gnostics not only by an involved mythology, but also by an insistence on an "ethics" of love. For Basilides,

---

3. See June Singer, *Androgyny, Toward a New Theory of Sexuality* (Garden City, New York: Anchor Press/Doubeday, 1976), 125 - 135.

4. G.S. Rousseau, Roy Porter, editors, *Sexual Underworlds of the Enlightenment* (Chapel Hill, University of North Carolina Press, 1988). See Rousseau's essay, 141; and Terry Castle's, 161, titled "The Culture of Travesty."

> The first precept 'of the will of God (is) to love everything, for everything is interrelated; and the second is not to desire anything; the third is not to hate anything.'[5]

General ethics tends to be dissolved in favor of a universal love.

This is a key factor in gnosticism. Metaphysics is the study of being and ontology; it is the study of the origin and nature of things. Gnosticism tends strongly to exaggerated metaphysical concerns and myths. On the other hand, it neglects ethics. To "love everything" means to love nothing, because all things are given equal status and equal meaninglessness. Gnosticism is metaphysics gone mad. The gnostic thinker could discourse on the powers of the three Principles (Light, Darkness, and Spirit) in a way that would indicate that we are getting a fundamental premise, only to lead us soon into other ideas apparently equally fundamental and as lacking in coherency.

Even more, an ethics is lacking in gnosticism. If everything is to be loved, and nothing hated, what is good and what is evil? Ethics means differentiation; it means that there is a difference between right and wrong, between truth and error. Gnostics like William Blake have embraced both heaven and hell, Christ and Satan. Giovanni Filoramo attempted to analyze the ethics of gnoticism on a particular issue: were they ascetics or were they libertines? They did despise the material realm, so in that sense they were ascetic by inclination. This, too, marked the Albigensians in medieval France. But, as the Albigensians concluded, if sexuality is nothing, indulgence is nothing, and only taking sexuality and marriage seriously is to be condemned, for the wise are ever taking "nothing" seriously. As Filoramo noted, the Gnostic Nag Hammadi texts contain no hint of immoral behavior.[6] He concluded, however,

> At the end of our gnostic odyssey, we find ourselves confronted by a final question frequently asked, but difficult to answer exhaustively or definitively. Isn't the

---

5. Giovanni Filoramo, *A History of Gnosticism* (Oxford, England: Basil Blackwell, 1990, 1991), 160.
6. *Ibid.*, 186.

> gnostic saved by nature? Isn't it precisely the awareness of this eternally preordained salvation that makes possible its ambivalent ethics, torn between two extremes: an asceticism that seeks to cancel out the very roots of our desires and a depraved antinomianism that mocks the laws of this world and its rulers?
>
> Perhaps Jonas was right to emphasize the anarchic and nihilistic character of a naturally rebellious ethics in search of a metaphysical liberty, which exists absolutely, in itself.[7]

What Filoramo graciously calls an "ambivalent ethics" is no ethics at all, because ethics cannot be ambivalent. It cannot say, Do not commit adultery, murder, or steal unless you really want to!

Over the Christian centuries, gnosticism has had many forms, notably the Paulicians, the Bogomils, and the Albigenses. It has also survived within Judaism and Islam. It has infiltrated Western philosophies and humanism as well. It was from the beginning anti-Christian, for, as Jean Doresse wrote, "they were in fact opposing Christianity by proposing a secret interpretation of it which claimed to be esoteric but was in reality distorted and factitious."[8] Would we not understand Gnosticism better by seeing it as an attempt to capture and subvert Christianity? Its appeal was its idiocy, and this was also its downfall with each attempt over the centuries to capture the minds of men. Its appeal has been the claim to special and secret knowledge; it offers the secret history of the universe and man, but never a plan for dominion, nor a world mission of salvation. Its detailed and precise myths were a means of over-awing the simple-minded. Their very extensive and precise details were, in reality, a means of imprecision, because no logical coherency existed.

Gnosticism often began with a "comforting" fact for sinners. "God" himself had fallen and was seeking to extricate Himself

---

7. *Ibid.*, 188.

8. Jean Doresse, *The Secret Books of the Egyptian Gnostics* (New York, N.Y.: The Viking Press, 1958, 1960), 302.

from an evil web of being. Well, if "God" is Himself fallen, who can condemn us for our sins?! And whose rules stand in so muddled a cosmos? Gnosticism was essentially antinomian because law and ethics simply diverted interest from their metaphysical concerns. At least to World War I, some insignificant groups of Paulicians survived within the Turkish Empire and were readily tolerated. To Christians, they were an insignificant, sniveling, and cowardly people and only potentially dangerous if they gained numbers or power because they were given to an "ethics" of hate! Their "morality" was to hate all the world equally!

Gnosticism often speaks of creation as the work of the fall of Sophia, Wisdom, into the world of darkness and matter. (This strand points to Iranian forms of thought.) The work, then, of the *Soter* or *Christus* is then to rescue the various scattered seeds of light. It is at this point that some scholars, like W. Crooke, spoke of "the ethical systems of Gnosticism ...grounded in the dualistic hypothesis."[9] Ethics, however, has meaning in terms of moral change or regeneration. The task of the "savior" in the gnostic system is not moral transformation nor regeneration, but simply separation of people from the world of matter. This is not morality, because the difference between the "good" seed and the "bad" seed is metaphysical, not moral. They *belong* to the world of light; they do not attain it by God's grace or by any other means.

We called attention to the importance of predestination and the gnostic antipathy to it. Let us look again at Swedenborg, a devout gnostic, who in *Angelic Wisdom Concerning the Divine Providence*, denied both predestination and salvation by God's grace. According to Swedenborg,

> 322. Sound reason declares that all men were predestined to heaven, and no one to hell; for all are born men, and in consequence the image of God is in them. The image of God in them is the ability to understand truth and to do

---

9. W. Crooke, "Gnosticism," in James Hastings, editor: *Encyclopedia of Religion and Ethics*, vol. VI (Edinburgh, Scotland: T. & T. Clark, 1913, 1937), 237.

good. The ability to understand truth is from the Divine wisdom, and the ability to do good is from the Divine love. This ability is the image of God, which remains in every sane man, and is not eradicated. From this comes his ability to become a civil and moral man; and the civil and moral man can also become spiritual, for the civil and moral is a receptacle of the spiritual. He is called a civil man who knows the laws of the kingdom wherein he is a citizen and lives according to them; and he is called a moral man who makes these laws his morals and his virtues, and from reason lives them. (2) It shall now be told how a civil and moral life is a receptacle of spiritual life: Live these laws, not only as civil and moral laws, but also as Divine laws, and you will be a spiritual man. Scarcely a nation exists so barbarous as not to have prohibited by laws murder, adultery with the wife of another, theft, false-witness, and injury to what is another's. The civil and moral man observes these laws, that he may be, or may seem to be, a good citizen; but if he does not also regard these laws as Divine he is merely a civil and moral natural man; while if he does also regard them as Divine he becomes a civil and moral spiritual man. The difference is that the latter is both a good citizen of the earthly kingdom and a good citizen of the earthly kingdom only, and not of the heavenly kingdom. The difference is seen in the goods they do; the goods done by civil and moral natural men are not in themselves good, for the man and the world are in them; the goods done by civil and moral spiritual men are good in themselves, because the Lord and heaven are in them. (3) From all this it can be seen that as every man was born that he might become a civil and moral natural man, so, too, he was born that he might become a civil and moral spiritual man; and this is done simply by his acknowledging God and not doing evil because it is against God, but doing good because it is accordant with God, whereby a spirit enters into this civil and moral activities, and they live; otherwise there is no spirit in them, and therefore they are not living. And this is why the natural man, however civilly and morally he may act, is called dead; but the spiritual man is called living. (4) It is of the Lord's Divine providence that every nation has some religion; and the primary thing in every religion is to acknowledge that there is a God, otherwise it

> is not called a religion; and every nation that lives according to its religion, that is, that refrains from doing evil because it is contrary to its good, receives something of the spiritual in its natural.[10]

If we strip Swedenborg's message of all its claims to revelations, what we have is a consistent humanism. It is not surprising that he influenced men like Kant and Goethe, who were hardly friends of revelation![11]

For Swedenborg, *all* men are "predestined to heaven." Every man's religion, whatever it may be, will provide him with the means of being a spiritual man. The term *God* has for Swedenborg a very different meaning than the Biblical one, and his "god" agrees with Swedenborg's humanism. We do not see Swedenborg humbling himself before the God of Scripture. Had Swedenborg openly stated his humanistic premises, he would today be remembered openly as one of the leaders of that faith. But, as a true gnostic, he sought to infiltrate and capture Christianity. The meager Swedenborgian movement that survives has a very limited number of churches, and with much money.

Under gnosticism, the State has never suffered. There is no challenge to its claims to sovereignty.

A final note: the resemblances between Swedenborg and Joseph Smith and Mormonism are more than coincidental. Smith was very much a child of Swedenborg.

---

10. Emanuel Swedenborg, *Angelic Wisdom Concerning the Divine Providence* (New York, N.Y.: Swedenborg Foundation, 1890, 1940), 326f.

11. Frank Sewall, "Swedenborg," in S.M. Jackson, editor: *The New Schaff-Herzog Encyclopedia of Religious Knowledge*, vol. XI (Grand Rapids, Michigan: Baker Book House, 1969 reprint), 188.

Chapter 21

Friedrich Nietzsche

Sadean man wants a successful world without God. His hunger for such a world is a consuming passion. Because of it, he will forgive anything else in an anti-God, anti-Christ country provided it is openly against the Lord. All kinds of evil in the Soviet Union and Red China were overlooked or forgiven because of their militancy against God. Mussolini and Hitler were equally anti-Christian in their beliefs, but their superficial compromises with the churches made them anathema. The growing hostility to Christianity became with many a dominant passion.

In European history, the Renaissance and the Enlightenment (with its fruits, Romanticism and Modernism) have been anti-God, but again not openly so. In the post World War II era, this anti-Christianism became more and more open, explicit, and aggressive. After World War I, there was a decade of dedicated immoralism, but, with the Great Depression, this lost its appeal. Its best literary expression was in the poetry of Edna St. Vincent Millay.

This anti-Christianism was aided by the studied irrelevance of the churches, both Protestant and Roman Catholic. Those which were modernist were not anything other than aliens in the temple, but the professing believers often equaled them in their damage. In the name of purity, one Protestant group does not permit participation in prayer if the leader is not of their group, i.e., Missouri Synod Lutheran, refusing to enter the dining hall until *after* the prayer. This is done even though the pastor praying is someone they came to hear because of his orthodoxy! In other churches, divisions take place over the issue of the "rapture," pre- or post-tribulation, and so on. The Roman Catholic circles, much attention is given to purported visions from Mary, which are amazing in their trifling nature. In one such "vision," dated June 12, 1976, Mary requires prayer with fingers together, pointing upward:

> My child, I am demonstrating the stance that Heaven expects of Our children in their prayer life. During the Holy Sacrifice there is much disrespect evident. You must, during the Sacrifice, place your hands together this way, and join in spirit with My son during his Sacrifice.

In another "vision" on July 25, 1974, Mary is said to declare,

> Shorts, slacks, shall not be worn in the presence of My Son! There will be no rationalization accepted for the commission of these acts of impurity.[1]

This is not to say that the anti-Christians are not commonly very stupid, but the sad part of the matter is that we are plainly told that the unconditional answer of God to prayers for *wisdom* is to grant it (James 1:5). Very obviously, church people are not interested in asking God for wisdom. Since I was young, I have often urged people to pray for wisdom, with virtually no reaction or action on their part. People want things, not wisdom.

The French Revolution set as the goal of humanity the ideals of *Liberty, Fraternity and Equality*. In time, liberty and fraternity gave way to the demand for equality. Equality is a concept that brooks no rivals and, finally, no equals. It challenges the validity of all authority, because it insists that autonomous man cannot be bound by any rules except his

---

1. *Directives from Heaven*, Friday, September 20, 1991, 2.

own will. This militates against *freedom under law* in favor of anarchic, autonomous freedom. To be *under law* is to be either God and His law, or the state and its law. If a man's will is as valid as that of any group of men, or of God, man will declare his independence from *all* extraneous authorities. Moreover, there can be no fraternity with men who have their own sets of personal fiats and decrees. There can, then, be no legitimate state. According to R.P. Wolfe,

> If all men have a continuing obligation to achieve the highest degree of autonomy possible, then there would appear to be no state whose subjects have a moral obligation to obey its commands. Hence, the concept of a *de jure* legitimate state would appear to be vacuous, and philosophical anarchism would seem to be the only reasonable political belief for an enlightened man.[2]

Of course, Wolfe's assumption that all men "have a continuing obligation to achieve the highest degree of autonomy as possible" is an amazing presupposition. It is like a man in the bright light of the sun insisting that all the light comes from his little candle.

However, modern man sees the world as something he must *remake* in order to capture it from God. He, therefore, makes many amazing statements in the course of his war. Charles Ives, for example, asks: "What has music to do with *sound*?" Well, what have words to do with meaning, or why should breathing be essential to life? When we challenge the *given* factors of life, there is no reason to stop at any point. We are then engaged in a radical deconstruction of all things.

Leo Steinberg sees all this as the great merit of modern art. In Wolfe's summary,

> For what in the world requires more courage than "to applaud the destruction of values which we still cherish?" Modern art always "projects itself into a twilight zone

---

2. R.P. Wolfe, *In Defense of Anarchism*, 1976, cited by David Miller: *Anarchism* (London, England: J.M. Dent, 1984), 27.

> where no values are fixed," he said. It is always born in anxiety."[3]

What de Sade recognized very clearly was the death of all values, which means the death of man and of all things because it means a war against God and against life. Life is created by God, and morality is the condition of man's life, so that to wage war against God and against morality is to wage war against life.

Friedrich Nietzsche (1844) saw clearly the lukewarm character of the Christianity of his day, but his solution was to abolish good and evil for a radically pragmatic view of life. Like his idol, Ralph Waldo Emerson, he wanted to transcend good and evil and make man free of all morality. *Beyond Good and Evil* (1885) began with his famous assault on truth:

> The falseness of an opinion is not for us any objection of it: it is here, perhaps, that our new language sounds most strangely. The question is, how far an opinion is life-furthering, life-preserving, species-preserving, perhaps species-rearing; and we are fundamentally inclined to maintain that the falsest opinions (to which the synthetic judgments *a priori* belong), are the most indispensable to us; that without a recognition of logical fictions, without a comparison of reality with the purely *imagined* world of the absolute and immutable, without a constant counterfeiting of the world by means of numbers, man could not live — that the renunciation of false opinions would be a renunciation of life, a negation of life. *To recognize untruth as a condition of life*: that is certainly to impugn the traditional ideas of value in a dangerous manner, and a philosophy which ventures to do so, has thereby alone placed itself beyond good and evil.[4]

Nietzsche's influence in the United States gained much from Emerson's preparatory work. In the 1930s, as a student, I witnessed the great popularity of Nietzsche's ideas, which faded outwardly as he was seen as a forerunner of Hitler.

---

3. Tom Wolfe, *The Painted Word* (New York, N.Y.: Farrar, Straus and Giroux, 1975), 91.
4. Friedrich Nietzsche: "Beyond Good and Evil," in *The Philosophy of Nietzsche*, chapter 1, sect. 4 (New York, N.Y.: Modern Library, n.d.), 4.

Nietzsche thus rejected living according to God and His law and truth. He also rejected the humanist's dream of living "according to Nature" as a fraud. He asked, "Why should you make a principle out of what you yourselves are, and must be?" Living according to Nature was actually a philosophy of self-justification. Nietzsche wrote,

> In your pride you wish to dictate your morals and ideals to Nature, to Nature herself, and to incorporate them therein; you insist that it shall be Nature "according to the Stoa," and would like everything to be made after your own image, as a vast, eternal glorification and generalism of Stoicism! With all your love for truth, you have forced yourselves so long, so persistently, and with such hypnotic rigidity to see Nature falsely, that is to say, Stoically, that you are no longer able to see it otherwise — and to crown all, some unfathomable superciliousness gives you the Bedlamite hope that because you are able to tyrannise over yourselves — Stoicism is self-tyranny — Nature will also allow herself to be tyrannised over: is not the Stoic a *part* of Nature? ... But this is an old and everlasting story: what happened in old times with the Stoics still happens to-day, as soon as over a philosophy begins to believe in itself. It always creates the world in its own image; it cannot do otherwise; philosophy is this tyrannical impulse itself, the most spiritual Will to Power, the will to "creation of the world," the will to the *causa prima.*[5]

Nietzsche ruthlessly exposed the compromising Christianity of his day and also the smug, compromising humanism and its virtual deification of Nature. Rather than self-preservation as "the cardinal instinct," Nietzsche declared that "life itself is Will to Power."[6] In this respect, Nietzsche was closer to orthodox Christianity as this point. Biblical faith sees all men as governed by their original sin, their will to be their own god (Gen. 3:5). Nietzsche's thinking is not only a militant and logical humanism, but it is also a clear recognition (and acceptance as a virtue) of the Biblical doctrine of man.

---

5. *Ibid.*, 8f; I, 9.
6. *Ibid.*, 14; I, 13

But for Nietzsche there was no truth. If a man seek it, "I wager he finds nothing."[7] What, then, can a man do? If the only reality is the impulse of a man, where does that leave us? Nietzsche's answer tells us that the only reality is what Christians call man's fallen nature.

> Granted, finally, that we succeeded in explaining our entire instinctual life as the development and ramification of one fundamental form of will — namely, the Will to Power, as *my* thesis puts it; granted that all organic functions could be traced back to this Will to Power, and that the solution of the problem of generation and nutrition — it is one problem — could also be found therein: one would thus have acquired the right to define *all* active force unequivocally as *Will to Power.* The world seen from within, the world defined and designated according to its "intelligible character" — it would simply be "Will to Power," and nothing else.[8]

Nietzsche was in effect issuing ultimatum to both churchmen and humanistic philosophers: Drop all your pompous pretensions and deal with man as he is, the naked Will to Power. Nietzsche immediately asks, "What? Does not that mean in popular language: God is disproved, but not the devil? On the contrary!"[9] The French Revolution, the culmination of the Enlightenment, was a "terrible farce" which scholars have interpreted to suit themselves "*until the text has disappeared under the interpretation*;" they have made their own "reality." "Everything that is profound loves the mask: the profoundest things have a hatred even of figure and likeness."[10]

The humanistic philosophers are unwilling to be open about their Will to Power. The Christians have sought to deal with it neurotically. For Nietzsche, "the religious neurosis" is "connected with three dangerous prescriptions as to regimen: solitude, fasting, and, sexual abstinence."[11] For Nietzsche,

---

7. *Ibid.*, 42: II, 35.
8. *Ibid.*, 43; II, 36.
9. *Ibid.*, 44, II, 37.
10. *Ibid.*, 45; II, 40.
11. *Ibid.*, 55; III, 47.

Christianity was a sick, neurotic pretension. Freud followed Nietzsche in this respect. For Nietzsche, both humanism and Christianity were pretensions in their moral claims: "There is no such thing as moral phenomena, but only a moral interpretation of phenomena."[12] To be beyond good and evil is to recognize that God is dead, and morality is a myth. Every system of morality is a tyranny against "nature" and against "reason."[13] A free world does not think in terms of Aristotle, or the Bible.

Nietzsche's thinking was leading him to an impossible conclusion, which, later in this thinking, destroyed him. If life is beyond good and evil, and there is no truth, then there is no reason to prefer life over death. He had concluded, "Morals as Timidity" best describes moral men.[14] Then why not *life as timidity*? He had allowed for no differentiation.

"*Morality in Europe at present is herding-animal morality*."[15] This was an easily made point. Most people usually follow a leader or a crowd. But what makes them better than Nietzsche, the truth? But Nietzsche has insisted that truth is a myth. Are the people wiser to bend to the popular ideas and advance themselves, or should they, like Nietzsche, arouse anger for exposing lies that are not really lies, since all things are meaningless? Should all argue with Nietzsche and commit suicide? Indeed, suicide in the latter part of the nineteenth century was becoming an intellectual practice. Nietzsche declared that mankind was becoming degenerate, brutalized into a "pigmy" and dwarfed.[16] Having rejected all standards, by what standard could Nietzsche say this?

Yet Nietzsche wanted philosophers *like himself* to enlighten humanity:

> *The real philosophers, however, are commanders and law-givers*; they say: "Thus *shall* it be!" They determine first

---

12. *Ibid.*, 80; IV, 108.
13. *Ibid.*, 97; IV, 108.
14. *Ibid.*, 107: IV, 197
15. *Ibid.*, 114f; IV, 202.
16. *Ibid.*, 117f; IV, 203.

> the Whither and the Why of mankind, and thereby set aside the previous labour of all philosophical workers, and all subjugators of the past — they grasp at the future with a creative hand, and whatever is and was, becomes for them thereby a means, an instrument, and a hammer. Their "knowing" is *creating*, their creating is a law-giving, their will to truth is — *Will to Power* — Are there at present such philosophies? Must there not be such philosophers some day? ...[17]

The answer is obvious: only Nietzsche. Such a person must believe in his own "virtues," i.e., have a "good conscience" about whatever he does.[18]

Nietzsche resented the morally superior man; it was to him a hateful form of elitism. He wanted an elitism based on amoralism, on the superman who is beyond good and evil, on a contempt for Christian morality. Moral judgment was anathema to Nietzsche. Morality was to him the "*uglifying*" of Europe, and especially a trait of women. Women were for Nietzsche a "possession, as confinable property."[19] The great need for him was "the rearing of a new ruling caste for Europe."[20] As against the prevailing slave-morality, there was a need, said Nietzsche, for a master-morality in which the rulers determine the conception of good. (This is now the Twentieth Century situation, the rulers of the state defining law and morality.)[21]

In 1887, in *The Genealogy of Morals*, Nietzsche further developed his argument. He charged the Jews with having created, in opposition to the aristocratic equation ("good=aristocratic=beautiful=happy=loved by the gods") another, with having insisted on a contrary one, "the wretched are alone the good; the poor, the weak, the lowly are alone the good; the suffering, the needy, the sick, the loathsome, are the only ones who are pious, the only ones who are blessed, for

17. *Ibid.*, 135f; VI, 211.
18. *Ibid.*, 141; VII, 214.
19. *Ibid.*, 166; VII, 238.
20. *Ibid.*, 186; VIII, 251.
21. *Ibid.*, 200ff; VIII, 260.

them alone is their salvation — but you, on the other hand, you aristocrats, you men of power, you are to all eternity, the evil, the horrible," etc.[22]

For Nietzsche, the Jews are the source of this false morality. The Church also carries on this evil: "The Church certainly is a crude and boorish institution, that is repugnant to an intelligence with any pretense at delicacy, to a really modern taste."[23]

In my university days, the students who openly affirmed Nietzsche's philosophy, (before Hitler made it less easy to do so), had a happy justification. By their contempt for sexual morality, their advocacy of cheating and dishonesty, and their rejection of "bourgeois" discipline, they were affirming their superior nature and the fact that their ways were the mark of a superior virtue. One student openly affirmed Nietzsche while still adhering to a Christian morality, a fact he justified with convoluted reasoning.

Nietzsche's hatred of God and morality had its penalty. God as the Creator of all life, and the Giver of the law, had made man in His own image. What hope could there be for a man so created? The walls were closing in on Nietzsche, and he concluded, "The sight of man now fatigues. What is present-day Nihilism if it is not *that*? We are tired of *man*."[24]

Man has a bad conscience because he is imprisoned by a Christian world and life view.

> I regard the bad conscience as the serious illness which man was bound to contract under the stress of the most radical change which he has ever experienced — that change, when he found himself finally imprisoned with the pale of society and peace.[25]

The logic of this is that man, the animal, must be freed from conscience so that he might kill, steal, and rape at will. This was an amazing statement from a weak professor! Did he

---

22. Nietzsche, *ibid.*; *The Genealogy of Morals*, First Essay, 13f.
23. *Ibid.*, 16f.; I, 9.
24. *Ibid.*, 26; I, 12.
25. *Ibid.*, II, 16; p. 76.

assume that the university would be a sacred precinct from the ravages of the new savage? Could he not imagine the obscene travesty of intellectual man that our politically-correct and crime-ridden schools have become? Abstract thinking can indeed be very dangerous.

For Nietzsche, "Undoubtedly the bad conscience is an illness, but an illness as pregnancy is an illness." It is an illness created by religion and will end with religion.[26] Mankind must realize it owes nothing to a mythical God. Redemption will come from superman, the "man of the future, who in this wise will redeem us from the old ideal." Assuredly, "this Antichrist and Nihilist, this conqueror of God and Nothingness – *he must one day come.*"[27]

In 1883, Nietzsche wrote *Thus Spake Zarathustra.* Here he affirmed, according to his sister Elizabeth Foster-Nietzsche, "All that proceeds from power is good, all that springs from weakness is bad."[28] Nietzsche saw Zarathustra as the first moralist and used him to destroy morality. It is a confused work, and yet its intention is clear: the death of God and morality, and the birth of superman. In terms of this,

> Once blasphemy against God was the greatest blasphemy; but God died, and therewith also those blasphemers. To blaspheme the earth is now the dreadfulest sin, and to rate the heart of the unknowable higher than the meaning of the earth![29]

Modern environmentalists are children of Nietzsche, although he would have despised them as he did everyone and everything. An undercurrent of *Thus Spake Zarathustra*, is Nietzsche's affirmation, not merely of superman and the death of God, but of the death of all men, of life. Like the Marquis de Sade, he was affirming that the ultimate "triumph" of anti-Christianity is the death of God and universal death. Even as Nietzsche hailed the superman, life as a dancing star, and more,

---

26. *Ibid.*, 81; 11; II, 19.
27. *Ibid.*, 92f; II, 24.
28. *Ibid.*, "Thus Spake Zarathustra," Introduction, 11.
29. *Ibid.*, "Thus Spake Zarathustra," Prologue, 3; 28.

he courted universal death and affirmed it. He was filled with *hatred.* He celebrated death in many ways. He glorified war and he celebrated the need to be ruthless. He exalted the contempt for a woman of a desert monk while frequenting prostitutes almost religiously. He held, "But I say unto you: your neighbour — love is your bad love of yourselves."[30] Man shall be trained for war, and woman for the recreation of the warrior: all else is folly." "Thou goest to women? Do not forget thy whip!"[31]

Now one of the falsest sources of information about Nietzsche was his sister Elizabeth Forster-Nietzsche, who said of her brother, that he "was a saint and incapable of carnal desire."[32] Lou Andreas-Salome used Nietzsche's call for a whip to keep women in the line against him. She had two philosophers who were madly in love with her assume the position of animals pulling a farm-cart. Paul Rees protested this humiliation, but Nietzsche "claimed that no other pose could more fittingly represent their relationship. He insisted that they be tied to the cart and Lou supplied with a whip." "Mr. Bonnet's camera caught the rapt ecstasy on Nietzsche's face." Apparently, Nietzsche had earlier used the statement about a whip for women; it was a few months later that he included the sentence in *Thus Spake Zarathustra.* By then, he was no longer in Lou's good graces.[33]

Nietzsche wrote, with the passing of time, books that were pseudo-Bibles. The language and format was a poor imitation of the Bible. His governing impulse can be seen by his vehement will to be his own, which is the Tempter's program in Genesis 3:5, every man his own god, determining good and evil for himself. He wrote,

---

30. *Ibid.*, 75; I, XVI.
31. *Ibid.*, 81; I, XVIII.
32. H.F. Peters, *My Sister, My Spouse, A Biography of Lou Andreas-Salome* (New York, N.Y.: W.W. Norton, 1962), 144.
33. H.F. Peters, *Zarathustra's Sister, The Case of Elizabeth and Friedrich Nietzsche* (New York, N.Y.: Crown Publishers, 1977), 59. For the picture itself, see H.F. Peters, *My Sister, My Spouse*, after 160.

> But that I may reveal my heart unto you, my friends: *if* there were no Gods, how could I endure it to be no God! *Therefore* there are no Gods.[34]

Nietzsche stated openly what many thought, and he brought about, in time, more plain speaking. The Death of God school of thought in the early 1970s (and basic to much since then) did not say, God is dead, but, rather God is dead to us; He no longer counts in our thinking.

Nietzsche held that God died out of pity for man.[35] Nietzsche himself had an intense love-hate relationship towards men. He wanted their recognition and adulation, and he hated them for worshipping other "gods" before him, that is, other men. He wanted men to forsake God and morality and to hail him as their deliverer. He insisted,

> Dare only to believe in yourselves — in yourselves and in your inward parts! He who doth not believe in himself always lieth.[36]

Thus Spake Zarathustra runs increasingly into madness. In the third part, one section is titled "On the Olive Mount." Five years later, he was signing his letters with Nietzsche Caesar, Dionysus, or the Crucified.[37] His syphilitic brain also led him to see himself as the Antichrist.

Meanwhile, he held, "man is something that must be surpassed."[38]

In *Ecce Homo*, 1888, an autobiographical essay, Nietzsche "proclaimed his immortality."[39] He saw himself as more learned and more clever than most people because he had no sense of sin.[40] He declared God to be "the greatest objection of Life."[41] Nietzsche recognized the explosive force of his thinking, and, in the essay, "Why I am a Fatality," he wrote:

---

34. Nietzsche, *op.cit.*, 98; II, XXIV.
35. *Ibid.*, 102; II, XXV.
36. *Ibid.*, 134; II, XXXVII.
37. Peters, *Zarathustra's Sister*, 107.
38. Nietzsche, "Thus Spake Zarathustra," in *op.cit.*, 204; III; IVI, 3, 4.
39. Peters, *Zarathustra's Sister*, viii.
40. Nietzsche, *op. cit.*, *Ecce Homo*, "Why I am so Clever," I, 32.
41. *Ibid.*, p. 34; 3.

> Hope is reborn with me. Thus, I am necessarily a Man of Destiny. For when Truth engages in struggle with the falsehood of ages, we must expect shocks and a series of earthquakes, with a rearrangement of hills and valleys, such as has never yet been dreamed of. This concept of "politics" is thus raised bodily into the realm of spiritual warfare. All the mighty forms of the old society are blown into space — for they all rest on falsehood: there will be wars, whose like have never been seen on earth before. Politics on a grand scale will date from me.[42]

He was right, of course, although more were involved in this revolution than he. Society was shifted from a religious foundation to a statist and pragmatic one. The modern State saw itself as beyond good and evil, as simply the power-center. Now only did the most terrible wars emerge, but "peace-time" became a nightmare. Crime increased as morality was despised. The human race, after Nietzsche, seemed determined to die like him, with sexually transmitted diseases.

Nietzsche held that "Christian morality is the most pernicious form of the will to falsehood, the real Circe of humanity, that has corrupted it."[43] But if we are beyond good and evil, all things are equal, and no standard for judgment remains. All the same, Nietzsche held that there should be a new form of dating, *Before Nietzsche*, and *After Neitzsche*:

> The unmasking of Christian morality is a unique event, a real catastrophe. He who throws light upon it is a *force majeure*, a fatality; he breaks the history of mankind in two. Man lives either before or after him.[44]

Nietzsche's goal was a more radical form of Voltaire's whose slogan, "Ecrasez l'infame!" he cites and then writes, "Have you understood me? *Dionysus* versus *Christ*."[45] But Dionysus gave him syphilis, a form of judgment! For him, Dionysus was the Antichrist.[46]

---

42. *Ibid.*, 134, Why I am a Fatality," 1.
43. *Ibid.*, 161; 7.
44. *Ibid.*, 143; 8.
45. *Ibid.*, 145; 8, 9.
46. *Ibid.*, "An Attempt at Self-Criticism," 156; 5.

H. Van Riessen, in his study *Nietzsche* (1960), very ably called attention to Nietzsche's problem. How can one deny God, deny truth, deny to man anything but an animal status, and still have any standard for any judgment? "Nietzsche could not believe in God, and he logically refused to recognize sin; indeed, he tried to build a culture based on sin."[47]

We cannot understand Nietzsche unless we see him in the line of Descartes, and, more proximately, of Kant and Hegel. The only real world is the world of ideas, of man's mental construction. Outer reality, if it exists, i.e., things in themselves, is unknowable. He could thus declare,

> It is of cardinal importance that the *real world* should be suppressed. It is of the most formidable inspirer of doubts, and depreciator of values, concerning the *world which we are*: it was our most dangerous *attempt* heretofore on the life of Life.
>
> War against all the hypotheses upon which a real world has been imagined. The notion that *moral values* are the *highest* values, belongs to this hypothesis.
>
> The superiority of the moral valuation would be refuted, if it could be shown to be the result of an *immoral* valuation — a specific case of real immorality: it would thus reduce itself to an *appearance*, and as an *appearance* it would cease from having any right to condemn appearance.[48]

Nietzsche had prefaced this with an existentialist affirmation: "there are no things-in-themselves!"

It is *very* important to understand what this means. Beginning with Rene Descartes, philosophy clarified its direction. Thomism had stressed Aristotle and had used him to "establish" a "proof" of the Biblical God. It had a mixed presupposition, God and man's reason as its starting point. But Descartes began with the autonomous human mind as his

---

47. H. Van Riessen, *Nietzsche* (Philadelphia, Pennsylvania: Presbyterian and Reformed Publishing Company, 1960), 47.

48. Friedrich Nietzsche, *The Will to Power in Science, Nature Society & Art* (The Metaphysical Need, B. New York, N.Y.: Frederick Publications, 1960), 84.

given or presupposition, and, with this point of ultimacy, went on to "prove" the existence of God and the physical universe. Between Descartes and Hume, the process of attrition led only one assured reality, the autonomous mind of man. How could one trust sense perceptions to report accurately on the outside world? The only trustworthy knowledge was, in some diminished sense, Descartes' starting point, I think, therefore I am, *cogito ergo sum*, the autonomous mind of man. This conclusion was seen as a threat to knowledge. But it did not occur to these philosophers to begin with God. Instead of, *In the beginning, God*, their premise was, In the beginning, the autonomous mind of man. By Nietzsche's day, Darwin had denied the need for God as Creator "scientifically." His thesis was illogical and racist, since he saw non-Europeans as less developed races. Darwin's "science" was a concoction of wild, irrational, and unscientific assumptions. Billions of years ago, in a cosmic void, a universe of nothing, an accident occurred, and an atom was created out of nothing. This means spontaneous generation, and the creation of something out of nothing, two unscientific assumptions and the wildest of "miracles." Then millions, perhaps billions, of miracles followed, until, with untold numbers of accidental changes, man and this present world appeared. Darwin recognized that such accidents could not create a seeing eye, but this did not deter him. Any preposterous miracle was preferable to God.

The philosophers were moving in the same direction: any answer other than God. The autonomous mind of man had to be ultimate rather than God. It was left to Immanuel Kant to replace both God and the physical world with the mind of man:

> Hitherto it has been assumed that all our knowledge must conform to objects. But all attempts to extend our knowledge of objects by establishing something in regard to them *a priori*, by means of concepts, have, on this assumption, ended in failure. We must therefore make trial whether we may not have more success in the tasks of metaphysics, if we suppose that the objects must conform

> to our knowledge. This would agree better with what is desired, namely, that it should be possible to have knowledge of objects *a priori*, determining something in regard to them prior to their being given. We should then be proceeding precisely on the lines of Copernicus' primary hypothesis. Failing of satisfactory progress in explaining the movements of the heavenly bodies on the supposition that they are revolved around the spectator, he tried whether he might not have better success if he made the spectator to revolve and the stars to remain at rest. A similar experiment can be tried in metaphysics, as regards the *intuition* of objects. If intuition must conform to the constitution of the objects, *I* do not see how we could know anything of the latter *a priori*; but if the object (as object of the senses) must conform to the constitution of the faculty of intuition, I have no difficulty in conceiving such a possibility.[49]

With such a premise, Jean-Paul Sartre could hold that God was irrelevant to his philosophy; his problem of knowledge was other people.

Philosophy and modern thought have come to the logical conclusion of their presupposition. The ultimate, if not sole reality, is the autonomous mind of man in its existential or momentary thinking, uninfluenced by God or man. What in some is insanity is in reflective men their basic philosophy. In Nietzsche, philosophy and madness met; the most logical conclusions were at one with his delusions.

For Nietzsche, there was no thing-in-itself, nor "a sense-in-self," nor "a meaning in itself."[50] Nietzsche, more radical than Kant, denied reality to Kant's distinction between *appearance* and any *thing in itself*.[51] We have ourselves created the world of values; thus, it follows, "All is false — everything is allowed!"[52] "To "humanise" the world means to feel ourselves ever more and more masters upon earth."[53]

---

49. Translator, Norman Kemp Smith, *Immanuel Kant's Critique of Pure Reason*, Kant's "Preface to Second Edition" (London, England: Macmillan, 1934), 16.
50. *Ibid.*, 63; I, i.
51. *Ibid.*, 63; I, i.
52. *Ibid.*, 102, l.

Nietzsche left the door open to "God" as the possible future point of maximum power. In a statement that points directly to the thought of the Jesuit scholar, Teilhard de Chardin, Nietzsche wrote:

> The only possible way of upholding the sense of the concept of "God" would be: to make *Him not* the motive force, but the condition of *maximum power*, an *epoch*; a point in the further development of the *Will to Power*, by means of which subsequent evolution just as much as former evolution — up to Him — could be explained.[54]

(To read Nietzsche is to realize how many moderns have "borrowed" his ideas! Many academicians are simply housebroken versions of Nietzsche.)

Nietzsche was opposed to the moral channels of life, such as love and marriage. He was "opposed to parliamentary government and the power of the press, because they are the means whereby cattle become masters." Also, he held, "The arming of the people means in the end the arming of the mob."[55] Given his exaltation of the will to power, Nietzsche despised the ideas of compassion, love, equality, and the like. People, he said, "demand freedom only when they have no power."[56] Like Sade, Nietzsche held, "*There is nothing else on earth but immoral intentions and action*," if we view things from the traditional and Christian perspectives, but, in reality, "there is no such think as a moral or an immoral action."[57]

The first of many books on Nietzsche that I read as a young man was George Burman Foster's *Friedrich Nietzsche* (1931). Foster, then "Late Professor of the Philosophy of Religion in the University of Chicago," clearly admired Nietzsche. He recognized Nietzsche's essential anarchism. Nietzsche, he held, was an autocrat whose goal was government by "reason and strength," for the fittest only.

---

53. *Ibid.*, 106; I.
54. *Ibid.*, 122; "The Will to Power in Nature," I.
55. *Ibid.*, 206; "The Will to Power as Exemplified in Society and the Individual," I.
56. *Ibid.*, 229; I.
57. *Ibid.*, 230; I.

> According to Nietzsche, the great man, the hero of the future, worthy to be master and ruler of men must necessarily be a criminal, — that is to say, a man who knows not good or bad, because he is above them; a man who is the scourge of humanity; a man who, in order to realize the expansion of his personality, needs humanity as a field of experiments, as a field in which he can sow suffering broadcast; a man warlike and hard-hearted...The aim of the Superman is a great aim; it is the realization of life in its fullness and entirety, in all its infinite possibilities.[58]

Foster, the modernist, found much to agree with in Nietzsche. He shared with Nietzsche his skepticism and unbelief with regard to Jesus Christ. Deussen wrote of the historical criticism which both he and Nietzsche, as students, found excellent.

> This same Deussen was speaking to Nietzsche on one occasion of the *Life of Jesus* which Strauss had just then published in a new edition, and expressed approval of the book. Nietzsche quickly replied: "The question is important; if you sacrifice Jesus, you must also sacrifice God."[59]

Nietzsche was right, and we can broaden his observation to say that once you sacrifice any aspect of the Biblical revelation, in time you will sacrifice all. You will then follow Nietzsche and de Sade in a hatred of all morality and life. Nietzsche, far more intelligent than the absurd Marquis de Sade, saw the conclusion and pursued it. Nietzsche died in 1900, at the beginning of a century he created, and a suicidal one, like himself.

If God is to be abandoned, and the moral life with Him, as Camus saw in *The Rebel*, then we must choose evil. By analogy, we must choose sickness and death instead of life. E. Michael Jones, in his excellent study, *Degenerate Moderns*, wrote:

> The prime anti-Western fantasy for our age, however, was expressed by Nietzsche. Two years after hearing the piano

---

58. George Burman Foster, *Friedrich Nietzsche* (New York, N.Y.: Macmillan, 1931), 83f.
59. *Ibid.*, 219.

> score of Wagner's epoch-making opera *Tristan and Isolde*, Nietzsche made a lifelong commitment to sexual revolution by deliberately infecting himself with syphilis in a Leipzig brothel. Thomas Mann saw in that gesture an act of "demonic consecration." Whatever the motivation, Nietzsche was outraged when Wagner had second thoughts. When Wagner "prostrated himself before the cross" by writing *Parsifal*, Nietzsche flew into a rage, not only against Wagner but against German music and all of Europe as well. Turning his disease-damaged eyes southward, he began to discern what he termed the "lewd melancholy" across the Mediterranean. As an antidote to Wagner's prostration before the cross, Nietzsche discovered Africa.[60]

Cornelius Van Til pointed out that one consequence of abandoning Christianity is *integration downward into the void*. This means "understanding" the man in terms of the child, the child in terms of the unconscious, the unconscious in terms of man's primordial and animal past, and so on. In the 1980s and 1990s, this means that political correctness attacks the whole Anglo-Saxon male in favor of women, blacks, and other races, provided that these other races are not too successful!

Nicholas A. Damask and Craig Cobane were two graduate students at the University of Cincinnati to be awarded Graduate Teaching Assistantships; a mandatory attendance at a "Teaching Effectiveness Workshop" followed. The sessions began with a "teacher"

> informing participants that all whites were racist and that blacks could not in any circumstances be racist. She stated that white men hold all power in society and that they oppress everyone: ethnic minorities, women, homosexuals, and the handicapped. Furthermore, she went so far at to say that the English language itself is constructed in a manner which makes it oppressive. Anecdotal evidence provided to prove this assertion included "good

---

60. E. Michal Jones, *Degenerate Moderns, Modernity as Rationalized Sexual Misbehavior* (San Francisco, California: Ignatius Press, 1993), 45.

> guys wear white, bad guys wear black," "stuck behind the eight-ball," and "blackmail," as well as many others.[61]

After this beginning, the sessions only went downhill.

What has happened to superman? All the assumptions Nietzsche called for are in place. Why do we see the triumph of the lowest common denominators, the "minority" people who will neither work nor study, the criminal, the political hacks, the moral degenerates, and so on and on? The "will to power" should have brought something "better" to the fore, if Nietzsche's thinking was sound. Precisely those things Nietzsche despised are not triumphing in his spirit, if not in his name. Why?

To eliminate God from your world-view is to eliminate history. If there be no good and evil, there is no premise for discrimination, then everything is meaningless. One would have to say that the proof of the "will to power" is to have power. This makes Wagner the victor over Nietzsche!

Albert William Levi observed, with respect to Sartre's Nietzschean existentialism, "The heart of Sartre's strategy for freedom is an attempt to destroy the decisiveness of the past."[62]

If it *could* be done, the destruction of the past would be a dangerous thing, for to destroy the past is to destroy conscience and history. Nietzsche, a man with a very bad conscience, tried to destroy or explain away conscience. In 1887, he published *The Genealogy of Morals*, as we have seen, but it failed to work for him; he could not erase morality nor his past. He was a man haunted by conscience and by history. History is the past of men and nations, but conscience is the past made ever present. Conscience means that man cannot escape himself and his history. But Nietzsche was determined to blot out religion and the past. Levi called this "a will to

---

61. Nicholas Damask and Craig Cobane, "Inside the Sensitivity Laboratory: Mind Control, Multcultural-Style," in *Campus*, Winter, 1994, vol. 5, no. 2, 3.

62. Albert William Levi, *Philosophy and the Modern World* (Bloomington, Indiana: Indiana University Press, 1959), 421.

illusion."[63] After all, Nietzsche *justified* the lie as necessary to life; he vindicated the will to illusion. In so doing, he placed himself into a strange contradiction to the will to power. The chronic use of the life that Nietzsche vindicated is a tool of weakness and of slaves, not of a superman. Moreover, Nietzsche's theory of the eternal recurrence, of an endlessly repetitive cycle of life, hardly means the triumph of superman. Triumph in history, from creation to the new creation, is true. Nietzsche sought to cut the ground out from under Christianity and ended up undermining his own foundations. In any war against God, man always ends up the loser.

John Neville Figgis reported, of Nietzsche's concept of the superman, that "an erudite Bavarian" once commented to him, "Every idiot fancies himself an *Übermensch*."[64] Nietzsche could, often correctly, ridicule the caricatures of Christianity that followed after German Pietism, and the thinking of Schleiermacher. Little did he realize what greater absurdities, sophomoric nonsense, and great evils would follow after him. His own life was full of ironies. The scholar, Paul Ree, influenced him greatly; they clashed over the love of Lou Andreas-Salome, and Ree was more successful than Nietzsche. Ree was Jewish. Then Nietzsche's sister, to his dismay, married a Jew.[65] Nietzsche was no lover of Jews. Most people experience frustrations and failures in their lifetime, but Nietzsche *experienced* everything as frustration and failure. "One quality he had — a terrific pride. He said that he was too proud to make friends, for none alive were of the same rank."[66] Life as superman can be very lonely.

Nietzsche was a classical scholar. He lived in an era when wisdom was located in Hellenic life, thought, and philosophy.[67] This severely limited his perspective. He was essentially ignorant of the Middle Ages and of the

---

63. *Ibid.*, 40, 58.
64. John Neville Figgis, *The Will to Freedom, or The Gospel of Nietzsche and the Gospel of Christ* (New York, N.Y.: Charles Scribner's Sons, 1917), 214.
65. *Ibid.*, 36-39.
66. *Ibid.*, 57.
67. *Ibid.*, 131.

Reformation; his view of the Bible was warped by Greek concepts which could never be successfully superimposed on the Scriptures. As a result, the Biblical view of God was repellent to him. The Greek idea of the supreme god, the god of Aristotle, was a transcendent being too great and too unmovable ever to condescend to create the world. In fact, for Hellenism as a whole, as Madigan has shown, "no god could touch matter and still remain a god."[68] For this reason, Gnosticism insisted that all creation and revelation was the work of a realm of powers below God, the demiurges. Nietzsche found distasteful the idea of a God concerned about humanity, about the incarnation and redemption of man as God's grace and love. Nietzsche mocked this Christian God and found it ironic that, when this God spoke to all the world in the New Testament, he spoke in Greek, and not too well, Nietzsche claimed. (Of course, the New Testament is Koine Greek, not the classical Greek of the philosophers and playwrights!)

There is a sad aspect to all of Nietzsche's attacks on Christianity. The academic world around him was politely indifferent to Christianity, for the most part. They were waiting for its quiet death and its disappearance into the past. As Figgis noted of Nietzsche, "He was not a man of the world."[69] In the Church's sense of the word, he was worldly, but he was not a man of the world. He sought disciples, not students. He spoke and lived intensely conscious of Christianity in a way other philosophers of his century were not. His hatred of Christ and Christianity was intense from first to last. He was like a renegade priest who fights the Church to his dying day. There are times when, in reading Nietzsche, one suspects, as did Figgis, that he hated it, not because he disbelieved it, but because he hated Jesus Christ.[70] Jesus Christ, as the antithesis of Dionysus, was to Nietzsche

---

68. Patrick Madigan, *Christian Revelation and the Completion of the Aristotelian Revolution* (Lanhan, Maryland: University Press of America, 1988), 83.
69. Figgis, *op.cit.*, 248.
70. *Ibid.*, 303.

the classicist the epitome of all that he detested. As a good Greek classicist, he helped re-create the priority of the State, and the Twentieth Century world wars over the articles of statist faith; the worst conflicts may well be ahead of us. No statues to Nietzsche will honor him for his part in shaping the Twentieth Century.

A final word: as I wrote the foregoing, a telephone call from a friend working with youth who live in the streets interrupted me. She reported a radical indifference to Christianity on the most part. Their intense interests were the theater and the dance. Life was not lived in the eyes of God but before men. Life was to them a stage for performance, a place for showing off. The world of Nietzsche had found some of its focus.

Chapter 22

Process Theology

But for the grace of God, one would have to say that mankind is afflicted with a terminal case of idiocy. It all goes back to Adam. There he was, in Paradise, standing next to a naked lady, Eve, and all he does is to munch on an apple, or whatever that piece of fruit was. Of course, Eve was no better. The first person she met with a smooth and promising offer led her astray. She was ready to listen to anyone except God and her husband.

Things have not improved since then. Breaking norms is a popular goal. What we get, for example, in the world of painting are "schools" like pop art, then op art, and so on. The world of scholarship is no better. We get slightly revised versions of old myths as soon as they are negated, and the newer schools of thoughts are really versions of the old follies.

Idiocies become us. In the town of Arcata, in northern California, feminists in 1993 organized a bare-breasted parade under the slogan, "Free your breast and your mind will follow."[1] Minds like that are better not freed.

---

1. Timothy Aepel, "Hip California Town Digs the Earth, Finds New Age Shangri-La," *The Wall Street Journal*, vol. CXXX, no. 50, Monday, March 16, 1994, 1, 5.

Process Theology is one step in the long development of theological modernism. It is the counterpart on the modernist side to what theistic evolution is on the evangelical side. Many evangelicals, eager to be in tune with science while maintaining a Biblical façade, insist on the validity of evolution with God guiding it in the background. By this means they hope to be scientifically acceptable while maintaining their evangelical status. It is, of course, an untenable position because it seeks to unite two mutually exclusive premises. Evolution's premise is chance, not God. Process Theology seeks to retain the form of Biblical faith while seeing the whole reality governed by the evolutionary process.

Two key figures in Process Theology have been Alfred North Whitehead and Pierre Teilhard de Chardin. A third can be added, Charles Hartshorne, in many respects the ablest man. Although very different from Karl Marx, he shared a common goal, to retain the form of Christian theism while giving it a different nature. With Barth, the façade was Biblical Christianity as against Modernism. With Hartshorne, it was theism rather than atheism.

In *Beyond Humanism, Essays in the New Philosophy of Nature* (1937), dedicated to William James and Charles S. Peirce, Hartshorne was critical of humanism. An able thinker, Hartshorne was not unfair in his critique of humanism, stating,

> Humanism is thus not so much atheism as a reinterpretation of God, not so much irreligion as an attempt to separate the sound human kernel of religion from its supernatural husks. It is the faith of humanists that the essential values of religion are independent of these husks. Thus Calverton speaks of "superior substitutes for religion and the gods."[2]

If religion is to be separated "from its supernatural husks," what remains will not be Christianity, nor historic theism. Hartshorne, in fact, is equally negative towards Christianity

---

2. Charles Hartshorne, *Beyond Humanism, Essays in the New Philosophy of Nature* (Chicago, Illinois: Willett, Clark, 1937), 2.

and humanism. "Supernaturalism and humanism are, I hold, two aspects of the same error, the mistaken notion that nature, in her non-human portions and character, is wholly subhuman."[3] Is there a third possibility, that nature, in some transcendent aspect, is God? This is the alternative Hartshorne is concerned with. It does not occur to him to question the existence of *nature*. Does *nature* exist, or is the term simply a collective noun for the sum total of the created order? It is easy to say that things natural exist, but does this mean that there is such an entity, entelechy, mind, purpose, or direction that can be called *Nature*?

For Hartshorne, fundamentalism does religion a disservice because it is, in its view of infallibility, "a meaningless idea" or "a positive evil."[4] His own view is better, he holds, "For just as God is nature as infinitely lovable, so he is nature as infinitely intelligible."[5] Nature as lovely and intelligible is a strange notion, and its key ideas are borrowed from the Biblical God. While holding to these ideas, Hartshorne rejected the idea that God is "externally issuing commands like a benevolent tyrant."[6] Hartshorne's god must be totally intelligible but never capable of an act or a command. He is simply "the hidden but always more or less dimly felt life of nature," (p. 27) a very safe god indeed, one who can never threaten man's position or stand. Such a god Hartshorne can love easily because he is never a threat, nor a judge; he has, in fact, nothing to say. Hartshorne recognizes that the Biblical God does impose restraints on immoral behavior, and a clear criterion of good and evil is needed. But for Hartshorne supernaturalism has a meager and tyrannical vision of being, and humanism is no better. According to Hartshorne,

> If God is simply "beyond" or outside of nature, then we know nothing of him and the very word "God" is meaningless. Similarly, with chance, or the relation

---

3. *Ibid.*, 3.
4. *Ibid.*, 8.
5. *Ibid.*, 23.
6. *Ibid.*, 26.

> between actuality and unrealized possibilities. What "may be" but is not cannot be withheld from actuality by any "inviolable" and eternal laws, for then it would not really be a "may be." We must find room for open alternatives *within* nature, just as we must, if we are to be theists, find room for God there.[7]

The presuppositions of this statement are revealing. God cannot for Hartshorne be outside of or beyond nature, because that would supposedly render *God* meaningless. He *must* be a part of the natural process, apparently. A supernatural God is meaningless because what is beyond nature cannot speak, nor give a revelation to those within nature because Hartshorne's presupposition is that nothing can exist outside nature, let alone speak. His dogmatism rules out the God of Scripture. For him there can be nothing real outside the evolutionary process. His concern is essentially to rule out naturalistic determinism. His "god" gives a certain freedom to the process to rescue it from a mechanistic and meaningless change. He is more interested in rescuing freedom for the mind than locating "good" as a person. He wants an organic rather than a mechanistic natural process. Thus for him, reducing mind and matter is essential.

Lynn Harold Hough observed, of Hartshorne's thesis,

> Doctor Hartshorne believes that the quantum mechanics has made possible a new synthesis in the terms of panpsychism. And he looks to Alfred North Whitehead as a particularly successful pioneer of the field. To put the result in a sentence, 'The new view consists of such a conception of God and such a conception of nature that the two coincide.' 'God is, according to the new theism, simply nature as literally and profoundly lovable, and not merely as pleasant to our senses or interesting for us to think about.' Doctor Hartshorne urges that we accept a theistic naturalism, understanding nature itself to be divine. The world is a world of body-mind. 'We shall never understand a God of love unless we conceive him as the all-sensitive mind of the world-body.' 'The new theism

7. *Ibid.*, 133.

> can perfectly well state its thesis as, 'the universe is divine,' that is, is the supremely integrated conscious organism.[8]

Hartshorne's god is not much of a god: we, he tells us, know *that* he is, not what he is.[9] When Hartshorne tries to discuss the "personality" of his god, his righteousness, or his purposes, he drifts into obscurantism. He wants a god who can evoke something resembling what the God of Scripture does, but without becoming that God.

In *The Gay Science*, Nietzsche said something most relevant to our subject: "without Hegel there could be no Darwin."[10] Without Hegel, there could be no Hartshorne either.

Very early, American Hegelians gave to process an infallibility and inerrancy of amazing character. Thus, Octavius Brooks Frothingham (1822-1895), a Harvard man, a Unitarian, and a leader in the new thought of his time, wrote:

> The interior spirit of any age is the spirit of God; and no faith can be living that has that spirit against it; no Church can be strong except that alliance. The life of the time appoints the creed of the time and modifies the establishment of the time.[11]

This deification of process, whether in Hegel, Marx, Frothingham, or Hartshorne may see itself as noble and wise, but it is a blueprint for tyranny. Tyranny, moreover, is called by a variety of names from the inevitable historical or dialectical process, to history, or by the term *god*. In every case, however well meaning, the implicit 'gospel' of this new god is a totalitarian order against which no man has a moral right to object or argue. "The life of the time appoints the creed of the time," and "no faith can be living that has that spirit against it." In other words, there can be no morally grounded or valid

---

8. Lynn Harold Hough, review, in *Religion in Life, A Christian Quarterly*, Winter number, 1938, 157f.

9. Charles Hartshorne, *Man's Vision of God, and the Logic of Theism* (Chicago, Illinois: Willett, Clark, 1941), 1332f.

10. Friedrich Nietzsche, *The Gay Science*, Book Five, 357, Walter Kaufmann translation. (New York, N.Y.: Random House, Vintage Books, 1974), 305.

11. Octavius Brooks Frothingham, *The Religion of Humanity* (New York, N.Y.: G.P. Putnam's Sons, third edition, 1875), 7f.

stand against the reigning tyranny that expresses "the interior spirit" of that age.

Nietzsche held, "Morality is herd instinct in the individual."[12] At the same time, he reduced consciousness to something that "does not really belong to man's individual existence but rather to his social or herd nature."[13]

Process theology implicitly eliminates both God and man.

W. Norman Pittinger called Hartshorne's version of Process Theology "a natural theology."[14] Process Theology is inevitably that because it allows no word to speak or to govern, other than a totally natural word. As a result, Process Theology spokesmen can give no word other than their own because none other, least of all God, are allowed to speak.

---

12. Nietzsche, *op. cit.*, Book Three, 116; 175.

13. *Ibid.*, Book V, 354; 299.

14. W. Norman Pittinger, "Process Thought: A Contemporary Trend in Theology," in Ewert H. Cousins, editor: *Process Theology, Basic Writings* (New York, N.Y.: Norman Press, 1971), 27.

Chapter 23

The Artificial Life

Lord Acton, in his *Lectures on the French Revolution* (1910), called attention to the fact Montesquieu, Voltaire, Turgot, Rousseau, and Diderot were all called "Liberal," but "The only thing common to them all is the disregard for liberty."[1] Too often, it takes only an anti-Christian position to qualify as a liberal.

France sought liberty *and* equality, two ideas that are in contradiction. To equalize men is to limit their freedom. The English system founded liberty on inequality, i.e., liberty could and does mean inequality. But, since the French Revolution, an increasing number of political movements have so stressed equality that liberty has been imperiled.

It was no accident that the French "Liberals" cited by Lord Acton had, despite very diverse political views, one thing in common, a separation from, or a disdain for orthodox, historic Christianity. They had "emancipated" minds. They were genteel members of the Enlightenment tradition.

---

1. John Emerich Edward Dalberg-Acton, *Lectures on the French Revolution* (London, England: Macmillan, 1910, 1925), 19.

The Marquis de Sade was a part of the same tradition, but he rebelled against maintaining the forms and declared open war on Christianity and its moral law. In fact, he declared war on all law in any form, saying, "what should we, who have no religion, do with laws?"[2] Sade did not deny the existence of God; he simply denied to God any jurisdiction over the natural realm. Hence, there could be no Christianity, no Biblical law, no law of any kind, only a total freedom for every desire or impulse. For Sade, "religion is incompatible with the libertarian system."[3] There could be no restraints on human freedom.

This Sadean doctrine has been advanced steadily since World War II with the legalization of abortion and homosexuality, and the increasing assault on laws governing morality. The death penalty is under attack, slander and libel laws are virtually dead, euthanasia is quietly and sometimes publicly practiced, and so on and on.

The radical and anarchic views of liberty which are increasingly advocated have as their premise the Sadean belief that it is criminal to resist Nature.[4] The Christian goal is supernatural man, the new man in Jesus Christ, whereas the humanistic perspective exalts natural man. What was once a criminal perspective is now a social and educational goal. This is an astonishing reversal of social policy for lawless activities now to have legal status and protection. Such a trend, if not reversed, will lead to the criminalization of Christianity and its laws.

World War II saw a dramatic change in the conduct of warfare in many ways, but certainly a major one was the use by war-time leaders of radio to influence the home front. Hitler, Churchill, and Roosevelt used radio consistently to influence people, and, with the Viet Nam War, Americans

---

2. Marquis de Sade, "Yet Another Effort, Frenchman," in *Philosophy in the Bedroom* (1975) in *The Complete Justine, Philosophy in the Bedroom, and Other Writings* (New York, N.Y.; Grove Press, 1965), 295.

3. *Ibid.*, 301.

4. *Ibid.*, 316.

were able to see American soldiers dying in battle. In the place of serious reflection, politics and war are now influenced by emotional reactions. Given the lack of serious, religiously premised thinking, the emotional impact of modern television has been very important in eroding the reflective nature required for sound conclusions.

In the early years of television, the most successful show was *Dragnet*, about two police detectives. There were no wild car chases, no shootings, nothing but quiet detective work. What has happened since is the replacement of such an approach with rapid action sensations. Having culturally replaced Christianity with naturalism, men have also replaced thought with sensations.

Dr. Cornelius Van Til spoke of the direction of such thinking. If man is explained, or seen primarily, in terms of his unconscious or subconscious, we explain man then in terms of the child, his primitive past, animals, and so on, so that what we have is *integration into the void.* This is the direction of society now, downward towards the void.

One of the casualties is sound thinking. In the name of naturalism, Sade practiced an anti-naturalism. Nature is marked by fertility, but Sade was anti-fertility, so his advocacy of things natural was governed by his hatred of God's purposes in creation. As we have seen, David Starkey, as a homosexual, advocated the artificial life, not the natural one. Nature, after all, while fallen, still reflects and is governed by God's sovereign will. It reflects God's order. Our Lord said, "Do men gather grapes of thorns, or figs of thistles?" (Matt. 7:16).

Now in Edna St. Vincent Millay, a superior American poetress of the twentieth century, a remarkable and sad development took place. In her very early poem, "Renascence," she identified God and nature and was clearly a nature-worshipper. Before long, however, as she embraced dissipation and sexual immorality, she parted company with nature. In *A Few Figs from Thistles* (1922), Millay directly attacked Christianity and Jesus Christ. In her "First Fig," she celebrated burning the candle on both ends. In her "Second Fig," she expressed scorn for the conclusion of the Sermon on the Mount, describing what was bulk "upon the solid rock" as "the ugly house," while her "shining palace (was) build upon the sand."

In *The Harp-Weaver and Other Poems* (1920), she expressed scorn on the built of people as "the fat of heart" (in "My heart, being hungry"). In *Second April* (1921), in speaking of death, her conclusion is

> "Life must go on;
> I just forget why."

Her goal, in Sonnet VII, is to "become accustomed to the dark." In Sonnet IX, she said, "I am the booth where Folly holds her fair."

In *Huntsman, What Quarry?* (1933), her growing love of death is much in evidence. How can anyone endure life, with its "Packed men and their hot rivalries," "Having smelt this grace, how cool it is?"

In *Wine From These Grapes* (also in *Collected Sonnets*, and *Collected Poems*). Millay had a series of sonnets entitled "Epitaph for the Race of Man." "Renascence" had become death instead. Earth for her was an "unhappy planet born to die." The "race of Adam," she wrote, would find "anonymous death," and "without a mind to monstrous Nothing yield your little breath;" man's achievement will be "destruction." Millay became one of a number of humanistic poets proclaiming a last judgment more ugly than ever preached by revivalists of old. Her humanism led her to despise man, as witness "My heart, being hungry." In *The Buck in the Snow*, the body in spoken of with irritation in "Moriturus" as "as best a bundle of aches." What we see in Millay is that the pose of a happy sinner, innocent in sin, does not produce a lusty sinner, but rather a sick and sour one.

In the 1920 census, it became apparent that the United States had changed from a rural to an urban nation. Some held that through the 1930s, most Americans were still being born in rural areas or towns under 5,000 in population, so that a rural-oriented culture still prevailed. In the 1920s and 1930s, this new, New York-centered culture was celebrated in *Vanity Fair*, which exalted the theatrical, the ephemeral, and the superficial.[5] This ephemeral culture soon led openly to the homosexual ethos openly celebrated. As far as the governing urban culture, and that of the media, was concerned, it was triumphant in its emphasis on the anti-moral and the artificial. Morality was declared to be alien to life, a religious imposition that should be discarded. The artificial life was thus radically anti-Christian as well as more or less anti-natural. The artificial life was an attempt to celebrate existence as against the fact of death, a *natural* occurrence.

The culture "at the top" in the Twentieth Century has been this anti-Christian culture of the artificial, a culture of death. When I was young, poetry was still a major part of everyone's schooling because it expressed the hope and faith of the people. Since World War II, poetry reaches a very small minority, and, without direct or indirect subsidies, we would see almost no poets.

Thus, Brooks Haxton, in *Dominion* (1986), held that "Left to our own devices, none of us Needs to believe in Hell. No one need believe" (in "Leaving the Drugstore for example"). The author may not believe in Hell, but his poems showed him living in it.

Bin Ramke, in *The Difference between Night and Day* (1778), like Miroslav Holub, finds the greatest emptiness in man. Edward Hirsch, in *For the Sleepwalkers* (1981), reeks with contempt for the common man with his normal life. William Meredith, in *The Cheer* (1980), wrote, "The love of living disturbs me," and he calls upon Freud to cure him (in "Dying Away").

---

5. Cleveland Amory, Frederic Bradlee, editors, *Vanity Fair, Selections...A Cavalcade of the 1920s and 1930s.* (New York, N.Y.: Viking Press, 1960).

The artificial life is all around, trying, in spite of our Lord's words, to pick figs from thistles and grapes from thorns. Of all such men, the words of Proverbs 8:36 still apply:

> But he that sinneth against me wrongeth his own soul: all they that hate me love death.

The artificial life begins with the hatred of God. Because it despises God's order, it seeks a radical leveling or equality. Because it hates men, it hates the equality it champions in order to choose death instead. Its goal is universal suicide.

Chapter 24

The Dream of Reason

With the Enlightenment, men's hopes for the future turned from God to Reason. Reason would, men believed, solve all problems and advance mankind to a new golden age. But the Enlightenment thinkers and *philosophers* already believed that a golden age had existed in Greece and in Rome, yet both cultures fell. As Frank E. Manuel pointed out,

> The apprehension of many eighteenth century *philosophes* over the internal decay of their society were reinforced by the haunting fear of another barbarian irruption from the heart of darkness that would overwhelm Western civilization in a repetition of the awful spectacle of the fall of the Roman Empire.[1]

Edward Gibbon wrote on *The Decline and Fall of the Roman Empire* as a warning of what could happen, and also to blame Christianity for destroying the Golden Age. In France, Diderot and others wrote the *Encyclopedia* with a like motive.

For the Christian, God cannot be overthrown nor supplanted, and therefore there is no cause for pessimism as to the ultimate outcome. As Psalm 2 tells us, the ungodly

1. Frank E. Manuel, *The Changing of the Gods* (Hanover, New Hampshire: University Press of New England, 1983), 93.

conspire together against God and His Messiah, but God laughs at their thinking; He holds them in derision. The psalmist counsels submission to God as the only way to escape God's judgment.

The Enlightenment substitutes for God its idea of inevitable *progress.* The French Revolution began the erosion of this faith, and World War I ended it. Current new world politics is the last gasp of such thinking, but with a difference. Instead of a natural evolution into a permanent Golden Age, it was now to be obtained only by revolutions, tortures, mass slave labor camps, and the like. The noble dream of reason had become a nightmare.

For Descartes, *reason* was a method, but, with time, man's contempt for this method was more in evidence than his trust in it. Reason was the property of the intellectuals, and they were increasingly held in contempt by others. Although the intellectuals created a refuge for themselves in the academic community, it was a fragile shelter. Great masses of peoples were given admission into that academic community, but the life of reason was not enhanced by this.

As a result, the life of reason became political correctness, not reason but coercion. As we have seen, Gertrude Himmelfarb has called attention to the shrill hostility to anyone who writes negatively about Stalin and his reign of terror. Moral judgments, and "judging Stalin," are coded "moral imperialism." Of course, these critics are deeply involved in moral judgments, and they are denying simply the right of judgment to Christian critics. The moral imperialism is on their part. They are in agreement with the Marquis de Sade that only Christian standards are untenable, and that all naturalistic ones are tenable.

The Enlightenment dream of progress was of an orderly development, building on the foundations laid by others who preceded us. But with the revolutionists who steadily replaced the Enlightenment thinkers, this sense of order was replaced with an insistence on disorder and discontinuity. Peter

Tkachev, who was the theoretician of revolution by professionally organized conspiracy, and who influenced Lenin, had as a basic premise that all Russians over age 25 be put to death "as incapable of moving with the times."[2] The American student movement of the 1960s had a related motto: "Never trust anyone over 30." This was a rejection of the past, and with it went a rejection of the family and an insistence on anarchic sexuality and morality.

The rejection of the past went hand in hand with a rejection of *reason.* The Enlightenment faith in reason gave way to an equally absurd belief in science and technology as the road to utopia. Lenin was an example of this. "In his own words, communism in Russia would be achieved when the whole country had access to electric power."[3] He said also, "Electricity will take the place of God."[4] This sounds very naïve to us, but it is hardly less so than the hopes routinely expressed today by politicians, educators, and scientists.

For the Christian, man is no less a sinner than he was a thousand or five thousand years ago. As Samuel Moffett commented, shortly after World War II, the invention of atomic power makes no more difference to man's moral problem than the invention of the bobby pin. But men idealize both the past and the possible humanistic future because God's version is anathema to them. Their dreams are anti-God and pagan. Poets have idealized the Irish pagan center, Tara[5], as did the novelist Margaret Mitchell, in *Gone With the Wind.* They believe that, if God could truly be made dead, then man would be free.

But man, while idealizing freedom, denies it in practice, and in our long history slavery and tyranny have been more in

---

2. Edmond Taylor, *The Fall of the Dynasties, The Collapse of the Old Order, 1905, 1922* (New York, N.Y.: Dorset Press, 1963, 1989), 53.

3. John Bradley, *The Russian Revolution* (New York, N.Y.: Exeter Books, 1988), 175.

4. Dimitri Volkoganov, *Lenin* (New York, N.Y.: The Free Press, 1994), 372.

5. J.N. Hillgarth, editor, *Christianity and Paganism, 350-750* (Philadelphia, Pennsylvania: University Pennsylvania Press, 1969, 1986), 118.

evidence than freedom. Man routinely indicts God by idealizing himself. Dante, in *Purgatory*, Canto Sixteen, has Marco Lombardo say,

> So if the present world is astray,
> seek the cause where it is in yourselves;
> and I shall give you now verified report.
> From the hand of the Creator who loves
> His work before it was being;
> the soul issues in perfect innocence,
> like a babe, which cries, laughs, frolics,
> knowing nothing but joy in its parent
> and turning gladly to what delights it.[6]

Dante here is a precursor of Rousseau; he does not give us a Christian perspective as does Paul, when he writes, "Yea, let God be true, but every man a liar" (Rom. 3:4). To indict God is to reject not only God, but any conceivable ultimate moral order.

The hostility to what the cultured despisers of Christianity call "moral imperialism" is an animosity to any ultimate moral order, i.e., one given by God. Man's original sin is to be his own god, knowing, or determining for himself, what is good and evil, law and morality (Gen. 3:5). Given this premise, it follows that moral autonomy becomes man's starting point. Autonomy means, literally, *self-law*, and, at the heart of the modern spirit is this intense religious conviction in man's autonomy. As Cornelius Van Til pointed out, "The idea of grace is wholly out of line with the idea of autonomous man."[7] Grace is the antithesis of autonomy, which is why the modern university and the church-related college give no place to grace. The curriculum of humanism too often prevails in both places, and grace is alien to the autonomous intellectual's view of scholarship.

---

6. Keena Wallis translation, in *American Aphrodite*, vol. five, number 18, 175, 1955.

7. Cornelius Van Til, *The New Modernism* (Philadelphia, Pennsylvania: The Presbyterian and Reformed Publishing Company, 1946), 84.

The premises of education are always religious, and, in our world, if they are not systematically Christian, they will be humanistic, as they are.

The doctrine of grace tells us that creation was God's gratuitous act, not necessitated in any way. Moreover, life is covenantal, and both the law of the covenant and its mercy represent God's grace. We are in all our being evidence of God's grace. As St. Paul says, in 1 Corinthians 4:7,

> For who maketh thee to differ from another? and what hast thou that thou didst not receive? now if thou didst receive it, why dost thou glory, as if thou hadst not received it?

The whole of the modern age, perhaps more so than previous ones because it has been so generously blessed by God's favors, is militantly anti-grace. The perspective of autonomy separates all spheres and all men and things from God, whereas the clear vision of grace is our total dependence on grace. But a world stripped of all grace would be no more than hell, and modern man's vision of life and the future is a hunger for hell. The Christian must separate himself from this disastrous goal. The dream of the Golden Age without God is a vision of hell.

Chapter 25

Exorcism

St. Paul, in Romans 6:1-2, raises and answers an important question:

> 1. What shall we say then? Shall we continue in sin, that grace may abound?
> 2. God forbid. How shall we, that are dead to sin, live any longer therein?

The question is one of exorcism. How shall sin be cast out of our lives? History is littered with attempted answers to this question, and it has been a frequent direct or indirect subject of fiction. The best known example is Robert Louis Stevenson's *Dr. Jekyll and Mr. Hyde* (1886). Stevenson in this work gives us an attempt to control or to exorcise evil. Dr. Jekyll, a scientist, creates Mr. Hyde, in itself an evil act which reveals a more than clinical interest in sin. Dr. Jekyll is confident that his virtue is so solid that he can explore evil and still control it. His simple-minded confidence in his own goodness in the end destroys both him and his creation. He could not exorcise evil by means of science, and evil exorcised life from Dr. Jekyll's being. The scientist, Dr. Jekyll, becomes progressively a devil because of his trust in his own goodness, his power, and his science.

In various forms, others since Stevenson have attempted to deal with the problem. One such effort was Lionel Rubinoff's *The Pornography of Power* (1967). Rubinoff's approach is existentialist. What this means is that his perspective is anti-theological; he reduces his concern to two central ideas, progress and power. Progress presupposes transcendental goals to govern history. For him, these are not God-given goals but man-made objectives. But the pursuit of truth has given way to the quest for power.[1] For Rubinoff, "Man is the being who makes himself by negating himself."[2] To the Christian, this can sound promising, but only if we see man negating his fallen nature. Rubinoff's viewpoint is very different, however. He writes,

> The main thesis of this book is that the most effective antidote for the performance of evil is the imagination of evil, and that the most viable therapy for the pathological abuse of power is, accordingly, an imaginative critique of power.[3]

We are thus faced with a variation of a theme by the Marquis de Sade.

For Rubinoff, transcendence is an act of imagination, not of grace. By giving in to the pornographic imagination, he can cleanse himself, and by indulging his power-hungry imagination, he can transcend it and become, apparently, an innocent lamb![4] The imagination of evil and of power supposedly enables man to transcend both. For Rubinoff, the humanistic imagination creates its own grace. Genesis 6:5 tells us of man that "every imagination of the thoughts of his heart was only evil continually." For Rubinoff, this evil imagination indulged is the road to salvation. Transcendence of evil comes through the imagination of evil.[5] If Rubinoff is right, then the prevalence of *Playboy* and *Penthouse* in the thirty years since he

---

1. Lionel Rubinoff, *The Pornography of Power* (New York, N.Y.: Ballantine Books, 1967, 1968), 2.
2. *Ibid.*, 3.
3. *Ibid.*, 4.
4. *Ibid.*, 89.
5. *Ibid.*, 200.

wrote his book should have us on the verge of a thoroughgoing age of sexual purity! He finds justification for this in Hegel's *Phenomenology of the Mind.*[6] His conclusion is this:

> The salvation of our age, then, lies in nothing less than the speed with which the *imaginative* celebration of evil can supersede the pornographic *enjoyment* of evil through the exercise of power.[7]

Rubinoff's thesis is not an incidental or unimportant one. In various forms, it is used to justify pornography, vindicate immoral television and film fare, and to vindicate the radical toleration of various evils.

We are living in an era where evil is more readily tolerated than virtue. In fact, *religious virtue* is denied validity and has been replaced by many with *scientific and rational virtue.* Rebecca West in 1945 reported on the opinion of an American scientist that the control of atomic power would only be safe in scientific hands. When asked what guarantee this gave of security,

> He, then, the least arrogant of men, replied by a simple claim that he and all his kind were born without sin. "How can you suppose that any scientist would do such a thing?" he asked, his spectacles shining with anger. "Science is reason. Why should people who live by reason suddenly become its enemy?" he put into words an implication which often can be recognized when Communist scientists write on other than technical matters. The comradeship of scientists with the Soviet Union, even if it amounts to a transference of national loyalty, cannot be wrong and cannot lead to any harm, because scientists cannot be wrong and cannot do harm, because they are scientists, and science is right.
>
> We are re-entering by a new door into the old world of fanaticism.[8]

In this perspective, evil is exorcised by science and reason.

---

6. *Ibid.*, 201f.
7. *Ibid.*, 201.
8. Rebecca West, *The New Meaning of Treason*, p. 173.(New York, N.Y.: The Viking Press, 1945, 1964), 173.

This exorcism requires, also, the separation of Christianity from education, politics, science, and society because it is seen as a corrupting and evil force.

We thus have evil redefined, and exorcism made into a necessary act against Christianity. In non-Christian thinking, evil is either denied, or, if affirmed, it is *a doctrine of selective depravity.* In this perspective, sin and evil are properties of certain groups only, black men, white men, Europeans, Asiatics, and so on. Selective depravity leads to simplistic solutions, i.e., eliminate the offending group, and all will be well.

As against this, the Biblical doctrine of *total depravity* declares that *all men* are fallen, of every race, creed, or color, and *all men* are saved only by the sovereign grace of Jesus Christ. Again, total depravity means that all of a man's being is totally controlled by his original sin, his will to be his own god, determining or knowing himself what constitutes good and evil, law and morality (Gen. 3:5). There are no degrees in man's fallen estate: it is total in all man, so that none can boast of any advantage over other men.

How, then, is the power of sin exorcised? Only by the sovereign grace of Jesus Christ through His act of atonement and His regenerating power in us. We are justified by His grace and made righteous judicially before God's judgment seat.

This act of grace must be followed by our sanctification, our growth in grace. Obedience to God's law-word is the way whereby we grow in His grace and service. Because we must not sin in the expectation that grace will abound (Rom. 6:1-2), we must rely on God's law for our sanctification, since it is His gift to us, an aspect of covenant grace, and an expression of His righteousness or justice.

The alternative to this is for man to pursue that program of the tempter as set forth in Genesis 3:5, to be his own god. More than a few contemporary writers have seen this as a legitimate goal.[9] This should not surprise us. It is the expression of man's

---

9. See John C. Lilly, M.D., *Simulations of God* (New York, N.Y.: Bantam Books, 1975, 1976), a favorable view; Ted Howard, Jeremy Rifkin, *Who Should Play God?* (New York, N.Y.: Dell Books, 1977, 1978), a critical but non-Christian view.

original sin, and it expresses the inner logic of humanism. Men like Jean Genet have seen sin as liberation. According to Richard N. Col, "To kill gratuitously, without hatred and without purpose, is a step in the right direction."[10] Moreover,

> To begin with, the act of murder is seen as an act of liberation — in every sense. Liberation from conventions, liberation from society, liberation from oneself and from God. It is the supreme act that destroys the *status quo*, whatever that may be.[11]

It is in terms of this that Jean-Paul Sartre saw Genet as *Saint Genet*, a saint of the existentialist world. Given this perspective, seen in popular forms of the media, the rise and prevalence of mindless, random, and unexplainable killings becomes understandable. They are forms of liberation, of exorcising the Biblical frame of reference.

Apart from the whole law-word of God, we can neither understand nor replace this evil form of exorcism, the exorcism of Christianity.

---

10. Richard N. Col, *The Vision of Jean Genet* (New York, N.Y.: Grove Press, 1968), 24.
11. *Ibid.*, 180.

Chapter 26

The Negation of God

In 1851, William Evert Gladstone (1809-1898), on a visit to the Kingdom of the Two Sicilies, saw with horror the rottenness of that realm, its contempt for justice, and its use of torture. He denounced that realms as "the negation of God erected into a system of government."[1] Now, more than in Gladstone's day, this phrase characterized many states. Unhappily, these are not simply backward states, but the one-time Christian nations of the West.

This "negation of God" begins in the churches with their antinomianism, their humanism, and their open contempt for Biblical religion. In November, 1995, there was the joint annual meeting of the American Academy of Religion, and the Society of Biblical Literature. Eight thousand professors of religion, Bible scholars, and Christian theologians met in Philadelphia, Pennsylvania to declare feminist, homosexual, and other aberrant views to be acceptable and preferable to orthodox Christianity.[2]

---

1. Cited by Malise Ruthven, *Torture, The Grand Conspiracy* (London, England: Weidenfeld & Nicolson, 1978), 159.
2. Peter Jones, "God Need Not Apply," in *World*, February 10, 1996, vol. 10, no. 85, 24-25.

We have today nations and their politicians dedicated to the negation of God with the dedicated assistance of many churchmen and churches.

The negation begins with the dismissal of belief in hell as religiously unworthy of religious belief. To reject belief in hell is to deny the need for justice. Hell tells us that justice has an essential and necessary place in the order of things because it represents the absolute righteousness or justice of all creation. To deny that there is a hell in the world to come means that man creates one in this world for all dissenters from the humanistic state. The Marxists have amply demonstrated this.

The negation of God means that because hell and justice are denied their ultimacy, then law too is denigrated. Law ceases to represent God's law order and becomes simply the arbitrary will of the State. The State as a law institution gives way to the state as a bureaucracy that sets its own rules and bends men to them.

The barren nature of the Conservative movement is apparent in its critiques of the left. It will confine itself to surface issues at best, not to their essential sources. If it criticizes *materialism*, it does so without reference to God, so that we have at most an ancient Hellenic idealism.[3] An unequivocal Biblical faith is seen as devoid of any intellectual status.

The modern State and the humanistic academic realm give us a telling example of the world of the Marquis de Sade without his openness. By evasion, and by claims to intellectual freedom, much literature has become a form of the Black Mass, a means of profanation. Sacrilege lends status to films, novels, dramas, and lectures. Because Paul in Romans 1:17-32 tells us that homosexuality is the expression of man's radical hatred of God, and of the burning out of man, homosexuals are given a place of great consideration and concern by apostate men both in and out of the Church. The desire of apostate man, as Jean-

---

3. See *The Intercollegiate Review*, Spring, 1996, vol. 31, no. 2 for an example of this.

Paul Sartre recognized in *Saint Genet*, is for absolute evil, a total purity of evil and a purity in the hatred of God.

Artists in particular have pursued this goal of profanation, blasphemy, and evil with intensity. Richard N. Col held that "to question values is the very birthright of the artist."[4] This means that the artist as a Sadean prophet dedicates himself to creating a new and radically meaningless world, in effect, to making a hell on earth.

The Biblical words for hell are *gehenna* or *hinnom*, or, the Valley of Hinnom, which was the city dump of Jerusalem. It was a place of fire and worms, the fire consuming the trash, and the worms devouring waste materials. A city dump is a place of miscellaneous objects, unrelated one to the other, and so an emblem of meaninglessness. *The negation of God is the negation of meaning.* Thus, as Jean-Paul Sartre's *No Exit* depicted, there is no true communication in hell, in essence only monologues.

John Milton, in *Paradise Lost*, has Satan declare when hurtled into hell,

> Which way I fly is Hell; myself am Hell;
> And in the lowest deep a lower deep
> Still threat'ning to devour me opens wide,
> To which the Hell I suffer seems a Heav'n.[5]

The damned for Milton are not only *in* hell, they *are* hell. Milton speaks of Satan as having "the hot Hell that in him always burns."[6] The damned are in hell because they are in all their being themselves a hell. Their being is a negation of God and, therefore, of meaning. In many, many leading persons in twentieth century art, in its various areas, this loss of meaning is very apparent, and often an increasing inability to function.

The same is true of other disciplines as they forsake meaning. John Peter Rumrich rightly observed, "For Milton, all

---

4. Richard N. Col, *The Vision of Jean Genet* (New York, N.Y.: Grove Press, 1968), 315.
5. Book IV, ll. 75-78.
6. Book IX, l. 467.

knowledge fears moral significance."[7] This is precisely what the modern academic scholar denies, any relationship between morality and knowledge. This premise leads to a denial of meaning to knowledge because it is morality that tells us what is good and evil. That which is neither good nor evil becomes before long meaningless to Sadean man. In fact, Sadean man denies meaning in order to eliminate any moral criteria.

The negation of meaning is also the negation of life. If nothing is either good or evil, and if all things are meaningless, then what difference is there between life and death? There is a proneness to suicide wherever such thinking prevails.

Conversely, the Bible tells us that with judgment "the books are opened" (Daniel 7:10), and Revelation refers again and again to the "Book of Life." There is with judgment a righting of all wrongs and an opening-up of the fullness of meaning, so that all factuality is seen as having God's total purpose in and behind it (Rom. 8:28). In heaven we see the totality of meaning, whereas in hell all meaning is negated because God is denied.

The negation of the triune God is thus more than an ecclesiastical concern because it follows from such a negation that life itself is rejected. The culture that pursues such a course is suicidal.

We thus live in an era when church and state, the school, academy, the arts, sciences, and more are engaged in a suicidal course of action. The general unconcern is an aspect of the will to death.

---

7. John Peter Rumrich, *Matter of Glory, A New Preface to Paradise Lost* (Pittsburgh, Pennsylvania: University of Pittsburgh Press, 1987), 72.

Chapter 27

Ethical Autism and Self-Absorption

Autism and artistic persons are relatively new to our culture. In particular, the Twentieth Century has seen an unusual amount of autism. It is of interest that, as the Twentieth Century has passed, dictionaries have given increasing space to the definition of this phenomenon. Thus, the *Webster's International Dictionary*, Second Edition, (1909), gives less space to the definition than does the smaller *Mirriam-Webster's Collegiate Dictionary* (1993), which reads,

> *autism*, n. (1912). 1: absorption in self-centered subjective mental activity (as daydreams, fantasies, delusions, and hallucinations) usu. accompanied by marked withdrawal from reality. 2: a mental disorder originating in infancy that is characterized by self-absorption, inability to interact socially, repetitive behavior, and language dysfunction.

We are most familiar with autism in children because it is most often reported in periodicals, but, when not overcome, continues indefinitely. Some families continue trying to overcome the total withdrawal of individuals aged thirty and more from speech and interaction with other persons. Aging mothers continue the painful task of caring for these autistic persons.

In previous eras, persons were at times seemingly autistic because some great shock or disaster shattered them to the point of incoherence, sometimes briefly, sometimes for years. This has occurred when the person has witnessed, when tied up, the brutal and horrifying torture of friends or sons, or the rape-murder of his wife and daughters. This is not the same as autism.

Autism is radical and even total subjectivism, and ours is the culmination of the thorough-going subjectivism of Romanticism. Art and life have been reduced to *self*-expression, and to convey an objective meaning has been derided by many artists, whether in painting, sculpture, literature, music, or in other spheres. To seek meaning in such works is held to be naïve: you must create your own, because meaning is subjective and personal. Lawrence Durrell, who favored all this, said, "The artist became an autist…he becomes a Selfist."[1]

An examination of modern art shows how clearly autistic it is, and the extent to which autism is exalted. Meaning is held to be purely personal, so that to strive for an objective meaning and frame of reference is held to be reactionary. Because it is an article of faith with true autism in art that God and morality are mythical, it follows that autistic art is alone tenable.

This, logically, is a development of original sin, of Genesis 3:5, where the tempter holds that every man should be his own god, knowing or determining for himself what constitutes good and evil, right and wrong, law and morality, or standards in any and every area of life and thought. Autism is a logical outcome of original sin.

An early "prophet" of autism was Oscar Wilde, a homosexual, and one who delighted in mocking established

---

1. Cited from Durrell's *The Key to Modern Poetry*, by Richard Pine, *The Dandy and the Herald* (New York, N.Y.: St. Martin's Press, 1988), 46.

learnings, conventions, and manners. The Arts took the lead in promoting autism in modern culture.

It is of interest that not all cultures have until now seen autism in their midst. Some cultures, whether non-Christian or superficially Christian, have been so outgoing in their ways that autism has been too alien to thrive.

Autism coincides with victimhood. In the Christian perspective, man's problem is *sin*. In humanism, as a developed form of original sin, man's problem is *victimhood*. Picasso's autistic art became socially relevant only with "Guernica," and the emphasis there was victimhood. In "Guernica" (1937), according to Elsen, "Picasso became deeply engrossed in the nonpolitical aspects of the project — notably the theme of the human deranged by pain." Despite Picasso's leftist politics, his painting "eliminated all political reference" and concentrated on human pain.[2] Picasso's political passion was superceded by his sense of victimhood. According to Elsen, "Grunewald's *Isenheim Crucifixion* was a source."[3] Now Grunewald attempted to depict the horrors of crucifixion in order to stress what the atonement cost Jesus Christ. But "Guernica" is not about atonement, simply about victimhood. Someone once referred to "Guernica" as a milestone in the history of art.

If so, it is a sorry milestone indeed, because for Picasso the only meaning is victimhood. Elsen, who thought highly of Picasso, still saw "Guernica" as sadistic.[4] Its horrors are overdone deliberately. Victimhood insists that there is no sorrow like unto its sorrow, and, if you fail to get the point, it is over-stressed to make sure that you will.

A relationship does exist between autism and sadism. What can we say about a 25-year old autistic man who subjects his loving mother to endless and humiliating work. His intelligence is of a high order, but he has withdrawn into

---

2. Albert E. Elsen, *Purposes of Art* (New York, N.Y.: Holt, Rinehart and Winston, 1962), 297f.

3. *Idem.*

4. *Ibid.*, 298.

himself. He is his own god and universe: this is the meaning of autism.

Culturally, autism is deeply embedded in Twentieth Century culture. One has only to read the Romantic poets to understand why we have autism in our time.

It is especially tragic that pietism has turned the churches into centers for the cultivation of autism. Nothing enrages many of these churchmen more than a challenge to their total self-absorption. They assume that Jesus came to enable them to be blessed in their autism. In *The Rebel*, Camus saw the purpose of Romanticism as the defiance of God and morality. The Romantics, from Byron and Shelley to our contemporary artists, have as their excuse the hatred of Christ. What is the excuse for these autistic church people?

We see all around us the rise of what is called "mindless" crime, and of "rebels without a cause." These terms only apply, if we seek an objective reference. This is denied by an autistic culture.

Chapter 28

Albert Schweitzer

In the early years of the Twentieth Century, it was widely held that the greatest Christian of the century was Albert Schweitzer (b. 1875). As a result, very early in the 1930s I began to read his works, on the gospels, on Bach, and, in particular, his *The Decay and Restoration of Civilization* (1932), *Civilization and Ethics* (1919), and *Indian Thought and its Development* (1936). What was very clear from these works was that Schweitzer, while an ordained pastor, made no pretense in his writings of being a Christian. His was a philosophy of the reverence for life, all life, so that it was a part of his ethics to rescue worms stranded on walk-ways after a rainstorm. Killing bacteria harmful to man was a problem to him, because it meant killing life, which was universally to be reverenced.

Schweitzer's thinking was hardly even post-Christian. It was Enlightenment logic carried to its reasonable conclusion. In *The Decay and Restoration of Civilization*, he saw rationalism as the spiritual maturity of man. "All real progress in the world is in the last analysis produced by rationalism."[1] For him, "The

[1] Albert Schweitzer, *The Decay and Restoration of Civilization* (New York, N.Y.: Macmillan, 1932), 88f.

ethical mysticism of reverence for life is rationalism, thought to a conclusion."[2] In *Civilization and Ethics*, Schweitzer held,

> In the matter of our relation to other men, the ethic of reverence for life throws upon us a responsibility so unlimited as to be terrifying.
>
> Here again it offers no rules about the extent of the self-maintenance which is allowable; again, it bids us in each case to come to terms with the absolute ethic of self-devotion. I have to decide in accordance with the responsibility of which I am conscious, how much of my life, my possessions, my rights, my happiness, my time, and my rest I must devote to others, and how much of them I may keep for myself.[3]
>
> A man is truly ethical only when he obeys the compulsion to help all life which he is able to assist, and shrinks from injuring anything that lives. He does not ask how far this or that life deserves one's interest as being valuable, nor, beyond that, whether and how far it can appreciate such interest. Life as such is sacred to him. He tears no leaf from a tree, plucks no flower, and takes care to crush no insect. If in summer he is working by lamplight, he prefers to keep the window shut and breathe a stuffy atmosphere rather than see one insect after another fall with singed wings upon his table.
>
> If he goes into the street after a shower and sees an earthworm which has strayed on to it, he bethinks himself that it must get dried up in the sun, if it does not get back soon enough to ground into which it can burrow, and so he lifts it from the deadly stone surface, and puts it on a puddle, he stops a moment in order to hold out a leaf or a stalk on which it can save itself.[4]

For Schweitzer, ethics is respecting the will to live of all living things as much as his own. Good morality is respecting the will to live of all other living things, bad morality is destroying life.[5]

---

2. Cited in Charles R. Joy, editor, *Albert Schweitzer, An Anthology* (Boston, Massachusetts, Beacon Press, 1955, 1960), 263.
3. Albert Schweitzer: *Civilization and Ethics* (London, England: A & Black, 1929), 258.
4. *Ibid.*, 247.
5. *Ibid.*, 246.

For Schweitzer, "Whatever is reasonable is good…To be truly rational is to become good."[6] But what is rational? It would appear that for Schweitzer it is the abandonment of orthodox Christianity for Renaissance and Enlightenment rationalism. He spoke favorably of both the Renaissance and the Eighteenth Century Illuminate.[7]

The question must thus be raised: wherein does Schweitzer differ from the Marquis de Sade? Sade began with the equality of all acts other than those motivated by a Biblical supernatural morality. For him, Christianity was the only evil and immoral form of life because it was anti-natural. Schweitzer's reverence for life does not call for Sade's studied immoralism, but it rests on the same uncritical reverence for all of life, and, implicitly, all kinds of activity. Now Schweitzer would no doubt have disagreed with Sade, but, having no doctrine of sin other than a lack of reverence for life, Schweitzer had no valid ground for a critique of Sade, for whom it was a pleasure in being hurt. This for them was life! Schweitzer did not use the word *sin*, but for him it, no doubt, meant a lack of reverence for life. For Sade, the reverence for life meant reverence for unfettered and free sexual expression.

Schweitzer's works are mainly badly dated, in particular his Biblical studies are very much irrelevant and have received no scholarly attention for many years and were of only brief concern in their day. On the other hand, his *Indian Thought and its Development* (1936), a much neglected work, is still relevant. Schweitzer found Far Eastern philosophies, most notably those of India, marked by a negation of life in their world views. Since basic to Schweitzer's philosophy and faith is the affirmation of and reverence for life, his analysis was a telling one. Because Eastern religious thought is marked by a negation of life, there is a lack of positive ethical action. Thus, the *Bhagavad-Gita* is marked by renunciation of the complete

---

6. C.R. Joy, *op. cit.*, 236.

7. Schweitzer, *The Decay and Restoration of Civilization*, 65.

maintenance of the difference between good and evil.[8] Indian thought has no consistent ethics of action, only an "ethics" of withdrawal which is a denial of the efficacy of ethics. For Schweitzer, whose ethics is one of action, i.e., the affirmation of life, Eastern thought is a dangerous surrender. But Schweitzer's problem is that his ethics has no real substance to it. Eastern thought negates life and seeks escape from it. Sade hated life and treated it with contempt. Schweitzer called for the reverence for life, but he had only his *personal* preference for this, no moral imperative. Moreover, since we live by eating, our reverence for life becomes a pragmatic matter: we do not ask the permission of plants and animals before eating them! Schweitzer's ethics of reverence for life leave all men guilt-ridden, if they practice it! This is hardly a good life-affirming view. Schweitzer's religion is not unlike that of Allen Ginsberg, for whom everything that lives was holy.

In *Out of My Life and Thought* (1948), Schweitzer said that "the great fault of all ethics hitherto" has been its limitation of ethics to the relations of man to man. Since Biblical law has laws dealing with the treatment of animals, plants, and waste materials, this is certainly not true. But the Bible lays down laws from God to man that govern God's property, i.e., man and all creation; it is God who is holy and therefore must be obeyed. For Schweitzer it is life that is holy, a very different perspective.

Schweitzer's ties thus are close to the environmentalists, the Gaia worshippers, the devotees of the exaltation of mother earth and nature above God and man. The whole focus of life is shifted. Thus, he wrote,

> I never go to a menagerie because I cannot endure the sight of the misery of the captive animals. The exhibiting of trained animals I abhor. What an amount of suffering and cruel punishment the poor creatures have to endure in

---

8. Albert Schweitzer, *Indian Thought and its Development* (New York, N.Y.: Henry Holt, 1936), 194f.

> order to give a few moments' pleasure to men devoid of all thought and feeling for them![9]

Schweitzer here sounds like opponents of the sale of furs, enemies of trained animal acts, and other of our present-day animal activists. For Schweitzer, everything that lives is sacred. He thus had no valid grounds with coping with the murder of men by men. To live was for him to incur guilt, and he could speak of "his tortured soul."[10] Despondency, estrangement, and pessimism marked his life.[11] He acknowledged his great debt to the Stoics.[12] Schweitzer's world was that of Charles Darwin. "A portrait of Charles Darwin hung on the wall of his room, rather than a likeness of Kant, Goethe, Zwingli, or Luther."[13] "He was in fact a thorough humanist."[14]

Schweitzer became a medical missionary to blacks in Africa. Since his death, he has fallen out of favor with many because of his supposed racism. In reality, what he manifested was a scholar's sense of superiority towards the uneducated. In actuality, he admired the African's sense of resignation to life. For Schweitzer, reverence for life was the basis of ethics. After that, most important was *resignation*, which he found common to "primitive cultures."[15] He held that "Resignation is the very basis of ethics."[16] This placed him close to Hindu thought! In fact, he went beyond many Hindus. "I never burn a field. Think of all the insects that perish in such a fire."[17] Perpetual guilt was basic to Schweitzer's view.[18]

---

9. Albert Schweitzer, *Memoirs of Childhood and Youth* (New York, N.Y.: Macmillan, 1931), 44f.
10. George Marshall and Daniel Poling, *Schweitzer, A Biography* (New York, N.Y.: *Albert Schweitzer Fellowship*, 1975), 263.
11. *Idem.*
12. *Ibid.*, 265.
13. *Ibid.*, 283.
14. *Ibid.*, 275.
15. Thomas Kiernan, *A Treasury of Albert Schweitzer* (New York, N.Y.: Gramercy Books, 1965), 63.
16. *Idem.*
17. Charles R. Joy and Melvin Arnold, *The Africa of Albert Schweitzer* (Boston, Massachusetts: Beacon Press, 1948), 74.
18. James Bentley, *Albert Schweitzer, the Enigma* (New York, N.Y.: Harper Collins, 1992).

W.F. Albright, in a review, saw Schweitzer's work as second-rate. His Biblical studies and his writings on Bach are not highly rated, nor his abilities as an organist. His pantheistic religion did not qualify him as an important thinker, a "pantheistic humanism," Albright called it. His ethics "is definitely in the Brahmin-Buddhist and not in the Christian tradition." His is an "ethical panvitalism of a rather naïve type." From the standpoint of medical science, Schweitzer's African medical mission ranked low. He also had an "aloofness from human suffering." For Albright, Schweitzer's *Philosophy of Civilization* "belongs definitely to the literature of philosophical escapism."[19] Albright's opinion is a fair one. Unhappily, men are not always influenced by the best thinking!

19. W.F. Albright, "Schweitzer and Civilization," in *The Hopkins Review*, Winter, 1950, 45-47.

Chapter 29

Paul Tillich

Paul Johannes Tillich (1886-1965) began his career as a Lutheran pastor (1912) and then as a chaplain in the German army in World War I. A professor of theology, he was dismissed by the Nazis in 1933 and came to Union Theological Seminary in New York, where he taught until 1955, and then at the Harvard Divinity School thereafter. An able lecturer, he was clear in his historical analyses of theology, but vague in stating his own.

Bertrand Russell, when asked how he ranked Schweitzer as a philosopher had answered, "It is news to me that he ranks as a philosopher at all."[1] This was an opinion that reflected the academic sense of monopoly on philosophy. On the other hand, Dr. Richard Friedmann of Schweitzer's Lambarene Hospital in Africa, in asking Paul Tillich of his opinion of Schweitzer, said it was

> a fact of life that the most important things we take for granted. What is most important to life, for instance? We talk about good food and water, but that which is most

---

[1]. Gerald McKnight, *Verdict on Schweitzer* (New York, N.Y.: John Day, 1964), 192.

> important which we would not survive for a few minutes without, sir, we hardly ever refer to. We take for granted the air we breathe, as we do the great germinal thinkers who have become basic to our entire systems of thought.[2]

This statement may have been simply graciousness on Tillich's part, but the element of truth was real. Tillich's thinking did presuppose forerunners like Schweitzer. The radicalness of Schweitzer was most appreciated by men outside the realm of Christian orthodoxy. When *Playboy* interviewed Schweitzer, the interviewer asked him about the radical nature of his reverence-for-life philosophy, and Schweitzer answered, "Who is to say which is the highest form of life and which is the lowest?" In other words, the flea and the rattlesnake are on par with man who for Schweitzer is not in God's image because there is no God. Schweitzer denied that Christianity was now a major world force. The human race, like all beings, had for Schweitzer, "an elemental goodness," but, unlike other creatures, man's goodness was "often largely submerged."[3] Paul Ramsey saw Tillich as the most ambitious and possibly greatest theologian in America since Jonathan Edwards.[4] On the other hand, Donald Grey Barnhouse did not see Tillich as a Christian thinker. For Tillich, Barnhouse pointed out, "Sin is not something one commits, but a sense of estrangement from one's true self." The Christian God is dead for Tillich; there is no God that man can relate to, and Tillich's God is beyond both being and non-being. Karl Barth gave to orthodox Christian doctrines a new content; Tillich went considerably beyond this to create a new terminology. Tillich was more a philosopher than a theologian, Barnhouse held, and an existentialist, "although we do not mind Tillich being an existentialist." "Tillich is trying to find his way in the darkness

---

2. George Marshall and David Poling, *Schweitzer, A Biography* (New York, N.Y.: Albert Schweitzer Fellowship, 1975), 276.
3. *Playboy*, December, 1963, 89, 90, 92.
4. Paul Ramsey, "The Keys to the Kingdom," *San Francisco* (California) *Examiner Book Week*, 1, 14; February 23, 1964.

of the world by a light which he insists on continually blowing out."[5]

Given Tillich's premises, a radical humanism, his "theology" is more sociology than anything else. At Union, his lectures drew an audience of auditors often very remote to theology and philosophy. He was a precise and able lecturer in dealing with the history of thought, but, where his own thinking was concerned, he often pushed language beyond the boundaries of meaning. His writing was clear enough: its meaning was obscure. Words were pushed into empty shells. Portentous meanings are implied, but it is all obfuscation because the content behind the words is next to nothing.

Tillich's alien content was apparent very early in an essay, "The World Situation." In the post-Reformation world, Tillich held that reason took on a new meaning, "a belief in reason." This was a new step. Now "Reason did not mean the process of reasoning, but the power of truth and justice embodied in man as man...a kin to the divine *logos*."[6] "Christian faith which proclaims Christ as 'Logos' cannot reject reason as the principle of truth and justice."[7] Tillich simply gives an existentialist meaning to the Logos and reason.

In 1948 Tillich's *The Shaking of the Foundations* was published, sermons given at the seminary with "A large part of the congregation at the Sunday services...from outside the Christian circle in the most radical sense of the phrase." Hence Tillich used another kind of language.[8] All the same, the sermons still echo an older homiletical style, although his reference to "the Christmas legend" and his citation of the resurrection of the *body* as a "symbol" indicated his modernism.[9]

---

5. Donald Grey Barnhouse, "What About Paul Tillich?" in *Eternity*, June, 1959, vol. 10, no. 6, 15-18, 46-48.

6. Paul Tillich, "The World Situation," in Henry P. Van Dusen, editor: *The Christian Answer* (New York, N.Y.: Charles Scribner's Sons, 1945), 2.

7. *Ibid.*, 44.

8. Paul Tillich, *The Shaking of the Foundations* (New York, N.Y.: Charles Scribner's Sons, 1948), preface.

9. *Ibid.*, 85.

In *Biblical Religion and the Search for Ultimate Reality* (1951-1952), Tillich says of man, and the concern he raises is a point basic to his thinking:

> If a man is that being who asks the question of being, he has and has not the being for which he asks. He is separated from it while belonging to it. Certainly we belong to being — its power is in us — otherwise we would not be. But we are also separated from it; we do not possess it fully. Our power of being is limited. We are a mixture of being and nonbeing. This is precisely what is meant when we say that we are finite. It is man in his finitude who asks the question of being.[10]

James Gutinann rightly observed that Tillich's existentialism owed much to Schelling and Romanticism.[11] For most of us, to have being is to exist. What does it mean to be a mixture of being and nonbeing?[12] For Tillich, it is "the ontological question, the root question of all philosophy." It is "the search for ultimate reality itself."[13] Does Tillich mean that we find God by searching ourselves? This is Romanticism indeed. Tillich invokes the I-Thou existentialist language, but the content is still not provided. It is evoked, but unspoken. Faith for Tillich is existentialist concern, something very alien to what St. Paul set forth.[14] We begin to understand Tillich's existentialist definition of being in his final lecture, when he states "that *being* and *person* are not contradicting concepts."[15] But where does that leave us when God is separated from being?

In 1952, Tillich's *The Courage to Be* was published. His starting point is this, "Courage as the universal and essential

---

10. Paul Tillich, *Biblical Religion and the Search for Ultimate Reality* (Chicago, Illinois: University of Chicago Press, 1955, 1963), 11. University of Virginia Lectures 1951-52.
11. James Gutinann, "Romanticism in Post-Kantian Philosophy," in Phillip E. Wiener, editor in chief: *Dictionary of the History of Ideas*, vol. IV (New York, N.Y.: Charles Scribner's Sons, 1974), 210f.
12. *Ibid.*, 11, 13.
13. *Ibid.*, 13.
14. *Ibid.*, 51-62.
15. *Ibid.*, 87.

self-affirmation of one's being is an ontological concept."[16] This statement tells us that we are indeed the world of Romanticism. Tillich's view of courage draws more from men like the Stoics and Nietzsche than it does from St. Paul because Tillich's idea of courage is based on existential loneliness, not Christian faith. It is related to his doctrine of anxiety over the prospect of non-being, and *anxiety* is an important aspect of Tillich's thinking. This tells us at once that he is an existentialist whose problem is non-being, not sin. Like others of this era, Tillich is less a part of the Christian world of life and thought than a parasite on it. Christianity still commands the churches, schools, and seminaries that make up a major share of the world of thought which is still independently financed and supported. As a result, many anti-Christian thinkers parade as Christians or as good churchmen in order to influence or command this powerful non-statist sphere. Whether Berdyaev in the Russian Church, or Tillich in the West, such men are only marginally related to the Christian faith. It should not surprise us then that Tillich has more to say about nonbeing, anxiety, and fear than about salvation and atonement. The central doctrines of Christianity are simply alien to him. When Tillich discusses guilt, his concern is existential, not soteriological. For him, "the courage to be" replaces salvation. For Tillich, grace can only have a "vitalistic interpretation," not a theological one.[17] In his *vitalism*, Tillich was fairer to Hitler and National Socialism than to the Bible. He at times borrows fig leaves from the Bible to cover his nakedness, but his efforts are failures. Both his concepts of being and nonbeing presuppose a world without the Biblical God. He summons us in fact to transcend theism by "absolute faith."[18] We are not in the Tillichian realm of gibberish as philosophy. His quest is "the God above God,"[19] i.e., above "the God of theism." His closing sentence in *The Courage to Be*

---

16. Paul Tillich, *The Courage to Be* (New Haven, Connecticut: Yale University Press, 1952), 3.
17. *Ibid.*, 85.
18. *Ibid.*, 185.
19. *Ibid.*, 186f.

is, "*The Courage to be is rooted in the God who appears when God has disappeared in the anxiety of doubt.*"[20] Great profundity, this!

In 1952 two scholars, Charles W. Kegley and Robert W. Bretall chose Tillich as the subject of the first volume of their symposium of *The Theology of Paul Tillich*, vol. I of "The Library of Living Theology." The authors tend to see Tillich as the greatest figure on the horizon of religious thought. He is even called a *theologian*; Tillich is no more a theologian than a physicist, but a loose use of language marks modernism.

John Herman Randall, Jr., in "The Ontology of Paul Tillich," calls attention to the fact that for Tillich "*knowledge* is ultimately a 'participation' in true being. This, I take it, is what 'existentialism' primarily means for him."[21] This is mysticism, not philosophy, nor theology. But Randall saw Tillich as an Augustinian! Randall quotes from an earlier syllabus of Tillich's, *A Complete History of Christian Thought* Tillich's statement was:

> Theonomy does not mean the acceptance of a divine law imposed on reason by a highest authority; it means autonomous reason united with its own depth...and actualized in obedience to its structural laws and to the power of its own inexhaustible ground. (85)[22]

Tillich, by his concept of *participation* in true being makes radical autonomous reason and theonomy mean the same thing! This acceptance of Tillich's mystical and existentialist confusion marks A.T. Mollegen's chapter on "Christological and Biblical Criticism in Tillich."[23] In terms of Twentieth Century thought, Tillich's thought is closer to phenomenologists like G. van der Leew's, *Religion in Essence and Manifestation* (1938) than to the Bible.

---

20. *Ibid.*, 199.
21. John Herman Randall, Jr., "The Ontology of Paul Tillich," in Charles W. Kegley and Robert W. Bartell, *The Theology of Paul Tillich* (New York, N.Y.: Macmillan, 1952), 134.
22. *Ibid.*, 144.
23. *Ibid.*, 229-245.

Tillich's vagueness certainly appears strongly in his chapel sermons published as *The New Being* (1955). If vagueness and imprecision is profundity, than these sermons are all very profound! He declared, "There is no condition for forgiveness."[24] What about repentance? Tillich loved to use such striking language. "Ethics may help us to a good life, but it cannot help us to truth. Religion may produce deep emotions, but it should not claim to have the truth. Only science gives us truth."[25] What relationship is there between such statements and the Bible? Is Tillich a new Bible? He gives to Jesus' statements in John's Gospel a new, existential meaning. In his sermon, "Is There Any Word from the Lord?", Tillich says that word does not come from the Bible or from Jesus Christ.[26]

Tillich's sermons in *The Shaking of the Foundations* and *The New Being* were followed by the collection titled, *The Eternal Now* (1963), fifteen sermons from 1956-1962. From 1933-1955, Tillich taught at Union Theological Seminary in New York, then at Harvard from 1955-1962, and in 1962 he went to the Divinity School of the University of Chicago, thus occupying chief seats among the modernist hierarchy of our time. The first sermon, "Loneliness and Solitude," reveals his intellectual bias clearly: it is an existentialist concern. For orthodox Christian is it sin, not loneliness, that is the problem. His concerns are essentially those of early Twentieth Century man, not man before God.

Tillich's *The Religious Situation*, which first appeared in English in 1932, German in 1926, was reprinted in 1956. Its basic premises had already gained currency, and the books reappearance accentuated them. Old meanings are rejected, but no new meanings emerge that are comprehensible. "Belief-realism" is stressed, but never clearly defined. Things "are to be studied for the sake of discovering what they signify for the

---

24. Paul Tillich, *The New Being* (New York, N.Y.: Charles Scribner's Sons, 1955), 9.
25. *Ibid.*, 66.
26. *Ibid.*, 114-124.

relation of our time to eternity. It is impossible, however, to do this unless we are virtually identified with them. Hence the limitation of all seriously meant statements about them."[27] Orthodox Christianity would say that our basic problem in understanding is a *moral* one, *sin*, whereas Tillich holds that it is *epistemological.* For Tillich, the problem man faces is, what is God, and, what is meaning? For historic Christianity, *the* problem is not God, but man, because he is a sinner. Tillich's perspective thus rejects the basic premises of theology. He sees *capitalism*, a *form* of economics, as a problem, perhaps the problem, whereas historic theology see *sin* as the problem. The focus from this perspective is salvation as the remedy whereas for Tillich it means the re-ordering of society. Tillich found fault with "the spirit of self-sufficient finitude" that he saw as marking capitalism and modern man,[28] but nowhere is that self-sufficiency more apparent than in Tillich, who defines God out of both being and non-being.

Dynamics of Faith (1957) is, like most of Tillich's works, a slender volume which suggests rather than expounds ideas. The God of Scripture speaks plainly because there is no unconscious element in His Being: a clean word is thus inescapable. Tillich's "God" and "theology" are beyond definition and hence vaguely expressed. For Tillich, the confusion begins with the very word *faith.* He begins very well: faith, like religion, is for him "ultimate concern."[29] What is the object, or the subject, of ultimate concern? The ultimate for him is beyond everything, and ultimate concern requires a doubt of all that is known or knowable. This is for Tillich the "Protestant principle."[30] Thus, faith is not what the Church has held it to be! Symbols and myth replace God as the objects of faith. Historic meanings are denied, and they are replaced with mystical vagueness. God is not needed by Tillich; "A

---

27. Paul Tillich, *The Religious Situation* (New York, N.Y.: Meridian, Living Age Books, 1932, 1956), 25f.
28. *Ibid.*, 218.
29. Paul Tillich, *Dynamics of Faith* (New York, N.Y.: Harper & Brothers, 1957), 1.
30. *Ibid.*, 29.

divine figure ceases to create reply, it ceases to be a common symbol and loses its power to move for action."[31] Why? Because Tillich so decrees it? For Tillich, "There is no faith without participation," a mystical doctrine.[32] Participation in what, in being or non-being? For Tillich, the object of faith seems to be faith, no more.

The fact that for Tillich God is a "problem" of anthropology and psychology, not theology, appeared clearly in a symposium, *In Search of God and Immortality* (1961), edited by J.S. Bixler. Tillich's chapter was on "The Idea of God as Affected by Modern Knowledge." Existentialism, having "revealed" man's predicament, has shown that the existence or non-existence of God is not the essential question, nor "the liberating answer." God's meaning is not in Himself, but in man's solutions to the meaning of life. God in Himself is of no concern, nor is He for Tillich "real."[33]

Tillich's Bampton Lectures at Columbia University appeared in 1963 as *Christianity and the Encounter of the World Religions*, four lectures, existentialist in perspective. From the human point of view, Tillich had only ably defined *religion* as ultimate concern, but the question then remains as to what the various *religions* are specifically. Here Tillich begins with amazing, unsupported conclusions. Thus, he says, "Both Protestantism and early Christianity can be called religions of the Spirit, free from apprehensive laws, and consequently, often without law altogether."[34] This is an amazing statement, a deconstruction of history and a blatant contempt of fiats. It is useless to follow Tillich's line of reasoning because it is a departure from reality. Is Tillich really concerned with world religions in any historical sense, or is it his purpose to fit his political and economic views into a world religious

---

31. *Ibid.*, 96.

32. *Ibid.*, 100.

33. Paul Tillich, "The Idea of God as Affected by Modern Knowledge," in Julius Seelye Bixter, etc.: *In Search of God and Immortality* (Boston, Massachusetts: Beacon Press, 1961. A Given Lecture, 1957), 100-109.

34. Paul Tillich, *Christianity and the Encounter of the World Religions* (New York, N.Y.: Columbia University Press), 10.

framework? In contrasting quasi-religions with religions in the proper sense, he seems to be determined to shift the meaning of religion to his private concerns. As usual too, Tillich's discussion reduces things to vague generalizations, i.e., the "two different ontological principles...behind (Buddhism and Christianity) as "identity" and "participation."[35] An intelligent discussion of Tillich's premises is difficult and absurd, like wrestling with an imaginary tar baby at times. His generalizations are sweeping and often absurd, as witness his comments on "Christian nature mysticism," Luther, etc.[36] There is a consistent thinness in his thinking. For the most part, his philosophy passes off water as soup.

In *Ultimate Concern, Tillich in Dialogue* (1965), D. Mackenzie Brown, then chairman of the Department of Religious Studies at the University of California in Santa Barbara, California, records the exchanges between Tillich and some seminar students. We are told at once by Brown that Tillich's God is beyond definition and knowledge. "This God cannot be said to exist or not to exist in the sense that we exist. Either statement is limiting."[37] God is supposedly too great for any such an approach.

Now the essence of Calvinism is that, while God is sovereign, He is also fully capable of self-revelation. The absolute creating and infallible God can only give an infallible word. Any other word is not God's word. Departures from this reformed view of Scripture require an incoherent and tentative God, and Tillich's "God" is not even that. Nothing survives of the Christian God, except the term.

More than a few of Dr. Brown's students wanted specific answers from Tillich, but his answers were marked by a studied vagueness and imprecision. Tillich recognized in passing "the important element of Calvinism — to subject the world to the will of God,"[38] but he was definitely not of that

---

35. *Ibid.*, 68.
36. *Ibid.*, 69.
37. D. Mackenzie Brown, *Ultimate Concern, Tillich in Dialogue* (New York, N.Y.: Harper & Row, 1965), 2.

persuasion. For Tillich, the doctrine of atonement, of Christ's substitutionary sacrifice of Himself for His people "is more or less dead."[39] Nothing in historic Biblical Christianity is at all alive and real for him.

Tillich makes clear that for him, "God" "is beyond existence or nonexistence."[40] If we see God "as a causality in the whole of the world," we have demonized him, Tillich held.[41] For Tillich, self-affirmation was a virtue, but it meant an affirmation of the infinite rather than the finite in us.[42] But was this not simply a way of exalting self? Tillich could say that "Christianity separated from Jesus as the Christ is an impossibility,"[43] but there was no agreement between the Biblical Jesus Christ and Tillich's existentialist reconstruction.

Tillich's *Theology of Culture* appeared 1959, edited by Robert C. Kimball. In this study, Tillich held that to begin, as theologians do, "with the assertion that there is a highest being called God, whose authoritative revelations they have received," is "more dangerous for religion than the so-called atheistic scientists." The idea of a higher being who gives people "information" about Himself is anathema to Tillich.[44] For him, "religion is an aspect of the human spirit."[45] Theology simply becomes, then, a form of anthropology. Existentialism for Tillich becomes a form of self-deification. As a result, he gives us, disguised as philosophy, more mysticism. Mysticism, whether in Schweitzer, Tillich, or a medieval nun, is a form of self-exaltation and ontological and metaphysical confusion. He discusses "symbols" which for him replace reality, so that Tillich remains forever in a cave, his world limited to shadows. For him, "religion is ambiguous" always, and to see a reality, an incarnation, or a true revelation

---

38. *Ibid.*, 129.
39. *Ibid.*, 147.
40. *Ibid.*, 167.
41. *Ibid.*, 169.
42. *Ibid.*, 205-207.
43. *Ibid.*, 217.
44. Paul Tillich, *Theology of Culture* (New York, N.Y.: Oxford University Press, 1959), 5.
45. *Idem.*

is to *demonize* religion. By going to Jerusalem to die, Jesus denied "the idolatrous tendency even with respect to himself."[46] Given this premise, Tillich reduces Christianity from an historical religion based on history to a series of myths so that culture is his substitute for history. Not surprisingly, he goes from seeing Jesus on His way to the cross to a survey of existentialist philosophers and philosophies. If Tillich has not been criticized more, it is because his critics have died of boredom. Tillich, like Schweitzer, has been a dead end in modernistic thought. Centuries earlier, Jacob Boehme had been a dead end of a like kind to Tillich, but more close to tradition. Tillich is full of references (vague ones) to concepts that barely appear in his writings, but seem to convey a catholicity of approach, as witness his *Love, Power, and Justice* (1954), with his citation of agape (Nygren's *Agape and Eros*), with his usual vague and generalized manner.

Tillich was a contributor to Simon Doniger's *The Nature of Men, in Theological and Psychological Perspective* (1962). His viewpoint was again existentialist, not theological. As a result, man's problem is not *sin* but *anxiety*.[47] Psychotherapy replaces salvation.[48] In discussing life after death, Tillich sees no *theological* or Biblical answer.[49]

This should not surprise us. In Japan, at Otani University of the Jodo Shin Sect Buddhist University in Kyoto June 6, 1960, Tillich was asked what would happen to Christianity if it could be proven that Jesus had not lived, and his answer was, "I say it would not mean anything."[50] Tillich's "Christianity" depends on Tillich, not Jesus. One Buddhist's response was, "Buddhism is not a system of doctrines but is primarily an

---

46. *Ibid.*, 66f.

47. In Simon Doniger, *The Nature of Man*, Paul Tillich, "Existentialism, Psychotherapy, and the Nature of Man." (New York, N.Y.: Harper, 1962), 42-52.

48. *Ibid.*, 171-182, "Human Nature Can Change A Symposium," Harold Kelman, Frederick A. Weiss, Paul Tillich, Karen Horney.

49. *Ibid.*, 201ff., Margaret Mead, "The Immortality of Man;" Tillich's comments are on 208-210.

50. "Dr. Tillich Encounters Japan," in *The Episcopal Overseas Mission Review*, Whitsuntide 1962, vol. VII, no. 3, 3.

experience, so all that matters in Buddhism is to have a Buddhist experience."[51] Tillich held to the "validity" of Buddhist "revelation" because "I believe there could not be special revelation if there were not universal revelation."[52] Tillich added, "I wouldn't speak to any Buddhist about the Lordship of Christ, because I wouldn't even say it to an American Christian."[53] Existential views and decisions were paramount to Tillich.

In Tillich's *Morality and Beyond* (1963), we have another slender work (95 pp.), where his negativity is again quickly exhausted. It is a Kantian work in that the reality of this God-created world is replaced by the construct of man's mind. Tillich begins by rejecting the idea that the gospel's message of "reconciliation and reunion with God as the Ground and Aim of our being," means atonement for sin. This for him transforms the gospel into "a multiplicity of laws;" instead of atonement for sin, Tillich wants a metaphysical, not a moral, reconciliation.[54] For Tillich, "The moral imperative is the command to become what one potentially is, a *person* within a community of persons."[55] Note what takes place in the name of "the moral imperative." To be a person means becoming one within a community. Now, in or out of community, morality is either good or bad: it is not identical with community as such because communities, like people, can be moral or immoral. For Tillich, "a moral act is not an act in obedience to an eternal law, human or divine." The moral act is "the inner law of our true being," which is hardly a belief in man's depravity! An "anti-moral act" is not the violation of a law, "but an act that contradicts the self-realization of the person as a person and drives toward disintegration."[56] Can anyone be convicted of theft or murder on such grounds?

---

51. *Ibid.*, 5.
52. *Ibid.*, 9.
53. *Ibid.*, 12.
54. Paul Tillich, *Morality and Beyond* (New York, N.Y.: Harper & Row, 1963), 13.
55. *Ibid.*, 19.
56. *Ibid.*, 20.

"The will of God" for us cannot be some eternal law. "The 'Will of God' for us is precisely our essential being with all its potentialities, our created nature declared as 'very good' by God in terms of the creation myth."[57] Tillich does not like Calvinism's reliance on Old Testament law, nor the term "total depravity," which he redefines existentially, and why not? Having redefined God, it is nothing for Tillich to redefine everything else![58]

Love is for Tillich the ultimate premise of morality, but it is an antinomian love, or *agape,* he affirms. This love or moral demand requires acknowledging "every being with personal potential as a person, being guided by the divine-human wisdom embodied in the moral laws of the past."[59] But laws in this sense are counsels only, not laws.

For Tillich, love means *equality*. Having said this, he finally admits the necessity for law and institutions to enforce the law.[60] His view thus replaces God's law with the law of the equalitarian state. What makes this law mean love when God's law does not? The Bible says, *God is love*, not the State.

Tillich's *The Future of Religions* was published in 1966, the year after his death in 1965. This slim volume includes tributes to Tillich by Jerald C. Brauer, Wilhelm Pauck, and Mircea Eliade. Tillich's four essays include one previously published in *The Journal of Bible and Religion* in 1965. These add little to his thinking.

In 1968, Tillich's *A History of Christian Thought* was published. In its earlier, mimeographed format, it went back to the World War II era. It is the most impressive of Tillich's works in that he shows therein clearly his familiarity with Christian thought over the centuries. His treatment was better by far than his passing references to Christian theologies in his many shorter works. In this study, he followed the disciplined tradition of German scholarship.

---

57. *Ibid.*, 24.
58. *Ibid.*, 35.
59. *Ibid.*, 46.
60. *Ibid.*, 93.

Tillich also was the author of *My Travel Diary, 1936* (1970), and *On the Boundary, An Autobiographical Sketch* (1964, 1966). In the latter, Tillich acknowledges his debt to Albert Schweitzer for his views on Jesus. In 1973, Rollo May's *Paulus, Reminiscences of a Friendship*, appeared. Tillich was a man who was sexually promiscuous, with an "inability" to be faithful.[61] According to May, a psychoanalyst, Tillich was sadistic.[62] He was aware of guilt, which he saw as "existentially universal,"[63] but not of personal sin, and he was known for his contempt for American "Puritanism" regarding sex. A mannerly old German, he was, in the words of one associate, capable of amazing coldness.

Like Schweitzer's, his influence diminished after his death, and with reason. Modernism was a mined-out view of thought, and its most prominent leaders most openly manifested the sterility of their thinking. There was a thinness of being in Tillich's thought that time has only made more abundantly clear.

---

61. Rollo May, *Paulus, Reminiscences of a Friendship* (New York, N.Y.: Harper & Row, 1973), 39f.
62. *Ibid.*, 62f.
63. *Ibid.*, 75.

Scripture Index

Index

The Author

Rousas John Rushdoony (1916-2001) was a well-known American scholar, writer, and author of over thirty books. He held B.A. and M.A. degrees from the University of California and received his theological training at the Pacific School of Religion. An ordained minister, he worked as a missionary among Paiute and Shoshone Indians as well as a pastor to two California churches. He founded the Chalcedon Foundation, an educational organization devoted to research, publishing, and cogent communication of a distinctively Christian scholarship to the world at large. His writing in the *Chalcedon Report* and his numerous books spawned a generation of believers active in reconstructing the world to the glory of Jesus Christ. He resided in Vallecito, California until his death, where he engaged in research, lecturing, and assisting others in developing programs to put the Christian Faith into action.

The Ministry of Chalcedon

CHALCEDON (kal•see•don) is a Christian educational organization devoted exclusively to research, publishing, and cogent communication of a distinctively Christian scholarship to the world at large. It makes available a variety of services and programs, all geared to the needs of interested ministers, scholars, and laymen who understand the propositions that Jesus Christ speaks to the mind as well as the heart, and that His claims extend beyond the narrow confines of the various institutional churches. We exist in order to support the efforts of all orthodox denominations and churches. Chalcedon derives its name from the great ecclesiastical Council of Chalcedon (A.D. 451), which produced the crucial Christological definition: "Therefore, following the holy Fathers, we all with one accord teach men to acknowledge one and the same Son, our Lord Jesus Christ, at once complete in Godhead and complete in manhood, truly God and truly man...." This formula directly challenges every false claim of divinity by any human institution: state, church, cult, school, or human assembly. Christ alone is both God and man, the unique link between heaven and earth. All human power is therefore derivative: Christ alone can announce that "All power is given unto me in heaven and in earth" (Matthew 28:18). Historically, the Chalcedonian creed is therefore the foundation of Western liberty, for it sets limits on all authoritarian human institutions by acknowledging the validity of the claims of the One who is the source of true human freedom (Galatians 5:1).

The *Chalcedon Report* is published monthly and is sent to all who request it. All gifts to Chalcedon are tax deductible.

Chalcedon
Box 158
Vallecito, CA 95251 U.S.A.